The Last Book I'll Ever Write

Parting Thoughts

related to our beach at "Northwinds"
Priest Lake, Idaho

Philip M. Hudson

Copyright 2022 by Philip M. Hudson.

Published 2022.

Printed in the United States of America.

All rights reserved.

No portion of this book may be reproduced, stored in a retrieval system, or transmitted in any form or by any means – electronic, mechanical, photocopy, recording, scanning, or other – except for brief quotations in critical reviews or articles, without the prior written permission of the author.

ISBN 978-1-957077-23-9

This book may be ordered from online bookstores.

Publishing Services by BookCrafters, Parker, Colorado.
www.bookcrafters.net

Table of Contents

Dedication..1
Preface..5
A Couple of Hundred Parting Thoughts...19
About The Author..223
By The Author...225
Author's Note..232
Vale..235

Dedication

This book is
dedicated to my wife Jan,
who has been the rudder of our
ship, and who has been encouraging
when we have faced strong currents and
powerful headwinds. She has been our keel,
preventing us from capsizing when we have
been knocked down by the foaming waves
that have streaked across our deck. She
has been our compass, showing us the
way when our course was uncertain.
She has been our chart, warning
us of hidden reefs and shoals,
and our barometer, alerting
us to impending storms.
She has been the wind
that has filled our
sails.

Preface

This,
my 62nd
book, is to be
shared by all, as
they sprinkle sand
and spread jewels on
our beach at Northwinds
and as they consider the
precious gemstones that
God has scattered across
the beaches of their
own lives.

With an ebb
and flow, an endless
cascade of waves caresses
the shore to tickle our toes, while
moonbeams ignite a thousand jewels
sparkling in the water at Northwinds. As
we gather together on our beach under a star
studded-studded sky, our smiles summon sweet
sensations, beckoning us to linger and to build
a castle in the sand. Deep within its keep, we
fastidiously nurture, fiercely protect, and
fondly embrace our precious memories
of family, who have gathered at
Priest Lake for four
generations.

It is with all
my love that I extend
to each of you an appeal
to enjoy this omnibus of my
parting thoughts. Embrace them at
face value or use them as springboards
to reach new heights of self-awareness as,
in your minds' eye, you navigate the waters
North of The Narrows that lead to our beach. As
we map out the shoreline of our lives, one day we
will all embark upon an adventure leading to an
undiscovered country from whose bourn none of
us will return. And yet, we have this consolation.
God's invitations have already been sent out to
each one of us, requesting our presence at a
reunion that promises to be celestial in
scale, and He has assured us that
there need be no empty seats
around His table.

Our family first came to Priest Lake in 1980, and we immediately fell in love. We bought our first boat, and trailered it to Coeur d'Alene, Pend Oreille, and Long Lake, as well as to the San Juan Islands, the Columbia River, Hayden Lake, Loon Lake, and others. But we kept coming back to Priest. The Eighties were spent camping at Lion Head (Mosquito Bay) and Kalispell Island, as well as Upper Priest Lake. In the early Nineties, we moved on to cabins at Hills' and Elkins' Resorts. While at Hill's in July 1994, we heard about a new development at Huckleberry Bay, and the rest, as they say, is history.

Over the course of a hectic week, we looked at all 46 lots along South Shores, but we kept coming back to lot #21, which had 135 feet of lake frontage and sat on a slight point of land with a beautiful view to the west, to the north, and to the south. In the summer months, it caught the last rays of the sun as it set at around 10:00 p.m. between Blacktail and Granite Mountains. The building site seemed ideal, and it wasn't hard for us to envision a cabin nestled among the Douglas Fir, Mountain Hemlock, Western Larch, Pacific Yew, and Wester Red Cedar.

We cleared a spot for a platform, which we soon built under Christopher's supervision. On it, we set up an "Elk Camping" tent which served us for 4 years. It had many of the comforts of home – a deck with cooking area, bench seating, and room inside for at least 6 cots. It kept us warm and dry in the shoulder seasons, and cool in the summer months. It was only occasionally visited by black bears, and squirrels only scampered across our sleeping bags once or twice.

We cleared a spot for a platform, which we soon built under Christopher's supervision. On it, we set up an "Elk Camping" tent which served us for 4 years. It had many of the comforts of home – a deck with cooking area, bench seating, and room inside for at least 6 cots. It kept us warm and dry in the shoulder seasons, and cool in the summer months. It was only occasionally visited by black bears, and squirrels only scampered across our sleeping bags once or twice.

In 1995, our 1,100 square foot dock was the first major improvement to the property, followed by our firepit area. For several years, our dock was the only one between East Twin Island and Two Mouth Creek. It was easy for boaters to find our camp site – "just go north and when you pass East Twin, ours is first (and only) dock." Our platform and tent made it easy to spot, as well. Locals from as far away as Coolin knew our dock, as well as our tent that could easily be seen as a bright white dot among the evergreens all the way from the entrance to the Thoroughfare five miles to the north.

In 1999, we got serious about building a cabin (or at least a garage, as we initially thought), so Tara and I started to work on the plans in earnest. At the time, she was living in San Francisco, so we sent lots of faxes back and forth, until we finally hammered out a design that we both liked. Basically, Jan was okay with anything we came up with, as long as there was a view of the lake from the kitchen, and after getting her green light on our proposal, we submitted the plans to a draftsman who produced a blueprint that we showed to a local builder.

Copper Bay Construction did the work through framing, after which we took over on the general contracting. Luckily, we were "dried-in" by November, when the first snows of winter blanketed the Idaho Panhandle. The entire project took about 9 months, from the summer of 1999 to April

2000. We went ahead and built both the garage and cabin at the same time, saving money in the long run. In the Spring and early Summer of 2000, we moved in – at about the same time that neighbors from Western Washington finished their cabin 10 lots down. We were the first ones to have cabins on the lake in Huckleberry Bay at South Shores.

At that time, we had no beach. Ours was a rocky and intimidating shoreline, to say the least. We spent the next 20 years creating, expanding, and improving our beach, and by 2022 it was pretty much completed – except for the annual restoration that has been repetitively necessary because of winter storms and spring runoff from the mountains. Most of the river rock on the beach and firepit area came from Two Mouth Creek, and was the product of endless trips with my pickups and RZRs. In the process, I went through two RZRs, two Toyota Tacomas, a Ford Ranger, and three Ford F 150s, not to mention three hernia operations and two hip replacements.

Our shoreline is particularly susceptible to North storms that pinwheel out of the Upper Priest Lake basin and come roaring down the lake from the entrance to the Thoroughfare before reaching us after traveling across 5 miles of open water. Three and four-foot wind driven waves hit our beach with spectacular effects – hence, it seemed natural to name our getaway at Priest Lake "Northwinds." Anyone who has experienced a storm North of The Narrows knows exactly why this is the perfect name for our cabin.

In addition to replenishing our beach with the sand we've brought in by hand – by my conservative estimate, at least a hundred yards – a few years ago we began noticing that Woodland Elves were depositing a wide variety of jewels both on our beach and in the water just off the shoreline and north of the dock. Grandkids have had a wonderful time collecting

these jewels, and diving for the ones in deep water. It seems that no matter how many they gather, more keep appearing, most frequently after a moonless night, when the Elves seem to have been most active.

It would be hard to imagine Northwinds without the beach. It's been a gathering place for our family for over a quarter of a century. Many of our grandchildren have received their "Master Roaster" S'mores Certification at our firepit. Unfortunately, my parents didn't have the chance to experience the beach or the firepit, although they enjoyed boating with us on Priest Lake from the early 80s to the mid 90s. But since then, three generations of our family have had countless memorable experiences at Northwinds. Babies have taken their first dip in the lake when only hours old, and in the depths of winter the brave few have taken polar plunges from our dock. In between, grandkids have taken their first swims in late June or early July, accompanied by the familiar expression: "It's really refreshing!" From Washington, to Oregon, Montana, Colorado, and Utah, our family has been drawn to Northwinds every summer, not to mention during the shoulder seasons, and at Christmas.

By late August, the temperature of the water can easily get up into the high seventies, and once or twice, it has even hit eighty degrees (at the surface). Some in our family have received their SCUBA certification at Priest Lake, and many have learned how to wake board, water ski, and wake surf North of The Narrows. We've witnessed the construction of dozens of cabins, and have seen many of their owners come and go. We've watched moose, bear, and deer, who have come for a closer look to see how we are managing our stewardship of their habitat, and we have used Northwinds as a launch point for countless motorcycle rides, hikes, and walks. We've watched grizzly bears teach their cubs how to forage for huckleberries in the Trapper Creek Drainage, and

we've (apprehensively) witnessed mama goats teach their babies to negotiate the slippery cliffs above Lion Creek. We've roasted thousands of marshmallows and have burned endless cords of wood at our firepit.

We've thrown (and lost) horseshoes at our pit and have spun dizzyingly on the tire swing to the point of nausea. We've endured dozens, and probably hundreds, of power outages, as well as a flood or two inside the cabin because of plumbing and septic problems. We've witnessed countless thunder and lightning storms from our deck and from the beach. We've marveled at the Aurora Borealis and meteor showers, and we've traced the path of the International Space Station as it has moved across the night sky.

We've shoveled tons of snow off our deck and have gone through many gallons of gas with our leaf-blower. We've popped a few tubes and gone after assorted paddles and kayaks that have floated north with the predominantly southern breeze, and we've thrown endless tennis balls out into the lake for our Golden Retrievers Katie, Danner, and Mackensie, as well as for other assorted dog-guests. Our three Goldens have been our lake dogs, and they've added another wonderful layer of dimension to our experience at Northwinds. All three have just needed to hear the word "Lake" to send them into a frenzy of excitement, as we've packed up the truck in preparation for the hour and forty-five-minute drive from home to the cabin.

Where else in the world can you drive 82 miles (on pavement) from your house with only three traffic lights between you and paradise? Directions to the lake are simple: Turn left at the light in Priest River and drive 41 miles to our gate. Along the way, you'll get to experience one of the longest driveways in the world. (OK – it's not quite that simple, but close.) One precaution though – don't forget the milk, bread, and eggs, because it's an hour-long round trip to the nearest market.

Our hot tub, outdoor shower, and sauna have worked overtime to accommodate the needs of all the grandkids, and the double pillow top mattresses and comforters in our bunk room have been a welcome retreat after a long day in the sun. "Too Hard", "Too Soft", and "Just Right" compete for favorite places to sleep in the North Loft. Air conditioning (in 2022) has made the dog days of summer more enjoyable, except in the basement, which always seems to remain at a constant 55 degrees, and our 22 KW generator and 400-amp service make the power outages much less inconvenient.

A dozen half barrels full of summer flowers brightens up the out of doors, and Having 4 red umbrellas on the deck, 4 more on the beach, and the potential for 4 more on the dock has made the noon day sun more bearable, and makes the deck, beach, and dock welcome gathering places.

The addition of ladders and diving platforms on the dock pilings, as well as 60 feet of Lilly Pad, defines our swimming area and guarantees endless fun! Two DUX boats and assorted inflatables and personal watercraft add spice to our experience. Transplanted trees have matured to the point that they need to be thinned on an annual basis to maintain our view from the cabin. Quaking aspen tremulously announce the arrival of even the slightest breeze from the south, and the daisy seeds that we scattered about years ago have finally germinated and are bursting with flowers. It's difficult to tell where the landscaping stops and the natural flora begins, but every summer now, it seems as if nature bursts with excitement at the arrival of endless waves of family.

Our "great room" is not so grand, but it is warm and comfortable, and is the perfect gathering place to accommodates a dozen or more of the family, who can be found there at any hour of the day or night. The design of our 26-foot-wide deck was a master stroke, and Christopher's chairs, benches, and tables have added a touch of class to its ambiance. Having the largest Blackstone Grill that money could buy, thanks to Ryan and Elizabeth, makes barbeques a favorite way to cook summer meals, and every time we clean up, I think of Mike and Kathryn's generosity in providing a state-of-the-art trash can in the kitchen! Children's laughter from the northwest corner of the deck reminds me that Kevin and Tara gifted their hot tub to the cabin, and Joanna's beautiful poem "Until We Built a Cabin" says it all from the wall beside our kitchen. (See page

226). Patrick and Kera's relief map of Priest Lake that graces our great room reminds us of dozens of excursions we've taken around both Priest Lake and the Upper Lake. Andrew's knick-knacks and décor accents have helped to make the cabin a warm and inviting getaway.

But, more than the "things" that have helped to make Northwinds special, it's all about the creation of memories. It's been an evolutionary process, but our cabin has been, and will continue to be, a memory-making machine, churning out individually tailored experiences that are all the richer for having been shared. We might have different takes on the same events, but when we whip up all their flavors into one smoothie, there is enough to go around for everyone, and it leaves each of us with a very pleasant lingering taste, while asking for more, please!

Huckleberry Daiquiris may escalate in price at the resorts around the lake, but it is the relationship capital at Northwinds that has continued to accumulate exponentially while straining neither our family bonds nor our individual budgets.

The sand on our beach and the jewels that are hidden within its grains are not the glue that has bound us together. But as we have been drawn to Northwinds, in our mind's eye it is nigh unto impossible to separate ourselves from the charisma of our beach. Because we have done it so many times, perhaps the entries in this volume will make it easier to envision ourselves together one more time, relaxing by the shoreline, soaking in the magic of the Crown Jewel of North Idaho, and sharing the experience of remaining in awe of God's creations.

A Couple of Hundred
Parting Thoughts

It's not the critics who count, nor those who point
out where the strong have stumbled or where the builders
of beaches could have made them better. No, the credit belongs
to those who stand squarely facing the water, whose brows are marred
by sand and sweat and blood, who have tried to create inviting opportunities
for their families to enjoy the wonders of nature, and have come up short again
and again. These understand the great enthusiasms and the grand devotions,
as they spend themselves in the worthy pursuit of this cause. However they fail
in their attempts to reach an accommodation with Mother Nature, at least they
have this consolation: They have fallen short while daring greatly, and so
their place will never be with those cold and timid souls who have known
neither victory nor defeat, nor acted upon their passion to craft with
nothing more than their own bare hands an inviting haven
along the shoreline of the unpredictable and tempest-
tossed paradise called Priest Lake. (Adapted from
remarks by Teddy Roosevelt
April 23, 1910).

Ashes to ashes and
dust to dust suggest the
inevitability of coming full
circle. We cast simple glass jewels
on our beach, but thru disproportion we
know that they will lose their luster due to
the wear of constant abrasion, just as we lose
ours as the vicissitudes of life grind down upon
us. We may sometimes feel that we are as rough
stones rolling, but through the Atonement, our
sparkle can be restored to a gemstone quality.
Now, go and scatter these jewels on our beach,
and by doing so, share with the world the
joyful news that God is great. Do it for
me, as well as for yourself, and
for all your brothers and
sisters on our Pale
Blue Dot.

An integral component of God's
landscape design is the vibrancy and vitality of
color. Its symmetry, beauty, and proportion are tools
with which we spread the joy and replenish the beaches of
our lives with His gemstones, whose sparkle helps us to see
beyond the veil that might otherwise insulate us from the
unreserved, unrestrained, unencumbered, uninhibited
compassion of our Savior Jesus Christ. Without their
adornment, we might forfeit the discipline of faith,
thereby blunting mortality's razor edge. God's
jewels are the currency we need to see and to
appreciate the sunrise, but more than that,
they are the multihued catalysts that
energize our capacity to introduce
to others the abundance of His

I'm
fairly certain that
the jewels you cast into
the water off our beach will
survive the wind and waves all
the way to the Millennium. In the
meantime, their sparkle will convey
a message of hope to the tired and poor,
to the huddled masses yearning to breathe
free, and to the refuse that has been cast upon
our inviting shoreline. These we welcome, the
homeless and the tempest-tossed, with lamps
held high beside the golden door. (See
Emma Lazarus, "The New
Colossus").

As Shelly's Ozymandias declared: "Look on my works ye mighty, and despair!" The sand that you now hold in the palm of your hand contains about a half million grains, but this pittance barely scratches the surface of God's creations. "Boundless and bare, (our) lone and level (beach) stretches far away."

All we
need to do is hold
these jewels in the palms
of our hands, or draw them
close to our hearts, to sense how
effortlessly they catch the Sun's
rays. As they attract and absorb an
even greater heavenly light, we find
ourselves irresistibly drawn to orient
our faces toward its cordiality. As
we immerse ourselves within its
luminosity, it washes over us,
confirming our faith and
infusing us with the
power of God.

The next summer storm
that comes pinwheeling out of the
north might easily wash your handful of sand
from the beach. (How many times has this happened
in the past!) But there is no wind so powerful that it can
completely erase its influence. None of us is an island unto
ourselves. We are a piece of the shoreline and a part of the main.
If a few grains be washed away by storms, we are the less,
as well as if the entire beach were. We are diminished
by any erosion at Northwinds, because we are
intertwined with the lake, and so, we never
"send to know for whom the bell tolls,"
for it tolls for each of us.
(John Donne).

When the time comes to scatter these few jewels on the beach, you will know that "I have come to the end of the road, and the sun has set for me. But I want no rites in a gloom-filled room. Why cry for a soul that's free? Miss me a little, but not too long, and not with your head bowed low. Remember the times that we once shared; miss me, but let me go. For this is the journey we all must take, and each must go alone. It's part of the Master's Plan for us, a step on the road back home. If you feel alone with a heavy heart, go to those we know and reminisce about our good times. Miss me, but let me go."
(Christina Rossetti).

Captain Jean Luc Picard declared: "Considering the marvelous complexity of the universe, its clockwork perfection, and its balance between gravitation, matter, energy, time, and dimension, I believe that our existence must go beyond Euclidean and other practical measuring systems, and that it is part of a reality beyond what we now understand." Perhaps, we should invite the captain to tarry with us on the beach at Northwinds, that he might quietly listen for the whisper of the Spirit that, on so many occasions, has spoken to our souls with the gentle reassurance: "Be still and know that I am God." (Psalms 46:10).

Oh, how I wish that the jewels we all
have found scattered across our beach and on
the bed of the lake could have included sapphires,
rubies, emeralds, and diamonds. In any case, I hope
that over the years grandma and I been able to spread a
few precious 'stones' of our own for our grandchildren
to discover at Northwinds. Perhaps our children can
now take up where we've left off. It may be time for
those who follow in our footsteps to become as
Woodland Elves, and help to preserve and
multiply the magic that has become
synonymous with our experience
at Priest Lake.

During
the long days
of summer, these few
grains of sand will absorb
heat from the sun. Our little
beach will be transformed into
a warm and inviting refuge
from what might otherwise
have felt like a cold and
forbidding world.

Scatter some of these
jewels across the beach, but
save a few, to be tossed into deep
water. Create a demanding situation
for those who will find and retrieve them.
In the process, as they are challenged to dig
deeply into their reserves and exert real effort,
they will begin to understand the significance
of the admonition that, in the conduct of their
lives, they will be happiest when they have
expended soul sweat, when perspiration
has preceded inspiration, and when
they have worn themselves
out in service.

I hope that
this little bag of
sand I've given you to
sprinkle on our beach will
make a small contribution to
the stability you seek in life. I
know we're supposed to build our
houses on a firm foundation, but
what is sand except bedrock that
has been ground down and
refined thru adversity?

Even a
thousand points of
light, although they be gathered
together, will still cast a very long
shadow. Not to worry, however, for in a
powerful demonstration of the universal
applicability of the law of opposition, if we
orient ourselves to that light, every apparition
of danger will remain behind us. If we take the
jewels that we have polished with the abrasive of
experience, and toss them about our beach or into
the water, some will surely catch the attention of
those with sharp young eyes, whose enthusiastic
minds are eager to embrace adventure. We hope
these gemstones will illuminate their darkest
of days and brighten their gloomiest paths
in the years to come, as they negotiate the
trail that we, God's faithful torchbearers,
have blazed for them during our own
travels along the highways and
the byways of life.

As I have carried
countless bags of sand down to
our beach over the course of more than a
quarter of a century, I've tried to remember
that, 'though I cannot do everything, I can do
something. I hope I helped build a little piece of
heaven here on earth, in this timeless corner of
North Idaho. But, compared to my own timid
efforts, I'm sure that you will accomplish
amazing things during your life, as
you shoulder burdens far heavier
than mine. Carpe diem!

Dozens or
even hundreds
of jewels may have
ended up on our beach,
but they personify only a
tiny fraction of our eternal
family. Where I'm going, I'm
certain we'll need name tags, at
least for a while. In any event, I'll
leave the light on for you! Don't be
in a hurry to return Home, though.
Spend God's precious gift of time to
remain anxiously engaged, and one
day you'll awaken to a sunrise that's
spectacularly celestial in its splendor,
and you'll discover that you've
miraculously found your
way Home, as well.

In the words of Thomas McCaulay: "To each of us upon this earth, death cometh soon or late. And how can we die better than facing fearful odds, for the ashes of our fathers and the temples of our gods," and for having deposited, with the currency of our blood, sweat, toil, and tears, grain upon grain of sand upon the beaches of our lives?

As you sprinkle these
Jewels on our beach, remember
that over the course of our lifetime,
Mom and I, thru our loved ones, have
been privileged to do something similar,
but with far greater significance. We have
been entrusted to cultivate an expanding
treasure of family gemstones that shine
within a small portion of a vineyard
that has been carefully nurtured
by the benevolent hand
of God.

Since
not every
yard of sand
of the beach upon
which we may find
ourselves during life's
journey contains golden
nuggets, our responsibility
is to discover the tiny flecks
that have been deftly sprinkled
among the detritus of life by the
providential hand of God and
then to recognize the silver
lining of celestial design
that surely exists in
every sow's ear.

When one
of these jewels that
you have cast upon our
beach catches a sunbeam
and then glints of gold or
red, orange, yellow, green,
blue, indigo, or violet, know
that, as it does so, it is only
refracting heaven's light,
and is sending a subtle
message that God is
never very far
away.

When we consider
the creation of our beach and
its maintenance and preservation,
we recognize that it has been a pitched
battle between me and Mother Nature. It is
one in which neither of us has ever conceded
defeat. My best assessment would be to say that
we've wrestled to a draw. In any event, I recall the
counsel of Teddy Roosevelt, who declared: "Far better
it is to dare mighty things, even though checkered by
failure, than to close ranks with those who neither enjoy
much nor suffer much because they live within a gray
twilight that knows neither victory nor defeat." ("The
Strenuous Life"). It is in that spirit that I ask you
to confidently scatter a handful of jewels upon
the beach for me, and to think positively,
even in the face of fierce storms that
might yet come out of the north,
as you journey thru life.

Sprinkle
this small bag of
sand on our beach, and
no matter how powerfully
the winds of adversity blow,
or how fiercely the tempests of
the adversary might pound upon
its shoreline, you will be confident
that you have done what you can to
fortify a little corner of heaven right
here at Huckleberry Bay, and that by
doing so you have anchored both it and
yourself to the infinite. These grains of
sand share a common characteristic
with thousands of points of light.
When taken together, they cast
a very long shadow. Their
influence is of infinite
proportion.

You are a precious
jewel in the eyes of our
Heavenly Father, and
you will always be
so, in my eyes,
as well.

When you have a
chance to be alone, and to sit
quietly on our beach, I want you
to toss a handful of jewels over your
shoulder as you reflect upon the hours
(days, weeks, months, & years) we spent
there. Remember that the beach has helped
hearts to love, blessed eyes to appreciate the
blinding light of the sun, and gifted our
spirits to cherish, not only the warm glow
of moonlight, but also the spectacular
smear of starlight from the Milky
Way, that, interestingly, we can
only see on the darkest
of nights.

No wind can blow
except it fills our sails. I hope
the contribution of sand that you
make to our little beach will help it to
stand until the Second Coming, when the
elements will melt with fervent heat, and its
grains will become as a sea of glass. There will
be reflected on its mirrored surface the visions of
glory, and in its depths we will catch a glimpse
of eternity. These will guide us along a charted
course that has been plotted by the stars, that
will lead us from Northwinds all the way
to the pillars of creation and the
gates of heaven.

Those who find themselves
in the awful grip of darkness because
they have refused to acknowledge the magical
light that steadily pulses from within the jewels
that have been scattered across our beach, may just
as well be adrift in the frigid vacuum of space. Their
habitations will eventually become desolate, forlorn, and
forsaken, as nature withholds her bounties. If we alienate
ourselves from God, all the world becomes our enemy, and
the Milky Way itself may seem a dark and a foreboding
expanse. Without the Light of Christ, the beaches of our
lives may be compared to raging interstellar seas and
galactic graveyards filled with strange dwarf stars,
fearful solar flares and terrifying supernova,
bursts of deadly gamma radiation, rogue
black holes, strange magnetars, and
the unrelenting horror of cosmic
cannibalism.

A bagful of sand may seem insignificant, and it could wash away in a storm, but if it does, not to worry. Sooner or later, some of its grains might find their way to Priest River, then to the Pend Oreille, then to the Columbia, and finally, to the Pacific Ocean. Who can say where their influence would end? Eventually, they could be scattered across the beaches of the world to remind us of the limitless reach of inspiration that comes from God.

Over the years, as we
and our beach at Northwinds were
slowly transformed, I often recalled the
words of William Mulock, whose example
taught me to remain at work with my hands
firmly on the plough and my face to the future.
Even as the shadows of evening lengthened about
me, the morning was always in my heart. With
him, I knew that the castle of enchantment was
always before me, allowing me to catch daily
glimpses of its battlements and its towers.
The best of life would always be further
on and would only briefly be hidden
from my eyes, existing as it does
somewhere beyond the hills
of time.

The colorful
jewels that dot our beach
remind us that we are not alone
in the universe. "The earth rolls upon
her wings, and the sun giveth his light by
day, and the moon giveth her light by night,
and the stars also give their light, as they roll
upon their wings in their glory, in the midst
of the power of God. Unto what shall I liken
these kingdoms, that ye may understand?
Behold, all these are kingdoms, and any
(one) who hath seen any or the least of
these hath seen God moving in
his majesty and power."
(D&C 88:42-47).

In a coming day,
this beach, our beach, including
the small bag of sand that you add to
it, will no longer remain in the possession
of our family, for the spirit that we have found
at Northwinds will return unto our God Who gave
it. But no-one can ever take this away from us: We've
all contributed to its beauty over the years and made
selfless investments in the enjoyment of the lake by
many people. No matter who upon these shores might
find the peace for which they have yearned, we will
always have this to remember: This was our land,
our home, and our sanctuary. Over the span of
four generations, our family laughed and we
cried here, and it was along this beach that
we forged the memories that are now our
heritage, that will last for time
and for all eternity.

Our
divine destiny was
envisioned by God during
our primordial childhood, it is
being molded in mortality, and it
will be established in eternity, when the
heavens will benevolently smile upon us.
We will be immersed in the matchless glory
of immortality and eternal life, and will inherit
thrones, dominions, principalities, and powers, in
an endless hierarchy of kingdoms that will render
noteworthy the symbolism of the scattering of jewels
across our beach. Into this tangible demonstration
of our faith, there could be woven any number
of allegorical interpretations that would
emphasize the profound significance
and potential of our noble
birthright.

Through the years,
and following every storm,
I tried to diligently ensure that
there would remain enough sand on
our beach to meet the challenges of a world
where stability seemed to be eroding before an
advancing flood of moral ambiguity and ethical
relativism. I replenished the sand, that there might
be enough for you to enjoy the company of your peers,
to embrace your fears, and to absorb your tears. In my
mind's eye, I envisioned a sanctuary where you could
find the peace that so often eludes us in the world,
where you could reconnect with nature, and
where God could gently remind you that,
as spring follows winter, and as day
follows night, the sun will come
out tomorrow, and when it
does, all will be well
in the world.

I have come to the
point where I realize that
what we get by reaching our
destination is not as important as
what we become during our struggle to
accomplish our objectives. We will surely
be dissatisfied if we trade what we need for
for what we want. It is our character, after all,
that nudges us off our status quo, and it is our
commitment that gets us moving. Finally, our
discipline and our resolve provide the energy to
boldly go where no mortal has gone before, to
travel among the stars. As I undertake that
journey, you can help. Where I am going,
I assume that dilithium crystals will be
in short supply, so take a handful of
the brightest jewels you can find
and scatter them on our beach.
Perhaps the greatest power in
the cosmos will then propel
me all the way to
heaven.

The billions of
grains of sand that make up
our beautiful beach absorb the Sun's
rays and are transformed into tiny power
dynamos that radiate a celestial energy. That's
one of the reasons why I was almost fanatical about
transforming Northwinds into a bit of heaven. Perhaps
naively, I thought that Mother Nature might realize that
my intentions were pure, and that She would then grant
me some accommodation. Being an optimist at heart, I
think that your contribution of a handful of sand
might yet influence Her to acknowledge and
posthumously reward my timid efforts.
Keep watching for Her sign that She
and I have come to terms. You'll
know it when you see it.

The
jewels
on our beach
remind us that
the soft glow that
we see when we raise
our eyes to behold the
stars within the heavens
above may be our one true
source of light, as we make
our way back Home on a
dark and dreary
night.

Ceaseless wave action
relentlessly pounds upon the
shoreline of our beach, continually
transforming its dimensions and its
composition. At one time, it might bring
in new sand, and at another, sweep away
that which had previously existed. The only
constant is that of change. We are all actors
who only briefly grace the world's stage, the
beaches of our lives. When we have mastered
the parts we have been groomed to play, and
we have tamed both the wind and the waves
to the best of our ability, we will move on
and embrace both new and challenging
opportunities. We will look forward to
an engagement with eternity that
completely immerses us within
a heavenly curriculum that
will expand to infinite
proportion.

From our
perspective at Northwinds, it is
our beach that lies at the center of the cosmos,
which makes your contribution to it of a handful
of jewels quite significant. Priest Lake has a way of
influencing us to venture outside the box. Others, who have
not experienced the quintessential Crown Jewel of North Idaho as
you have, tend to think small. When they do, they risk envisioning
themselves as insignificant beings condemned to live out their lives
on a Pale Blue Dot far out on the Orion Spur of the Milky Way,
26,000 light years from its galactic center. But consider this:
If only one in a thousand of its 200 billion stars supports
planets like Earth, that would leave 200 million worlds
within our galaxy alone sporting beaches just like
ours, nestled on the shores of mountain lakes of
equally pristine beauty. That isn't vain
repetition on the part of our Creator;
it's theatrical encore at its very
best. It's evidence of the
perfection of His
Creation.

If, through willful neglect, carelessness,
or inattention, the sixty-five feet of our beach at
Northwinds were to be left unattended for only a few
years, it would be indistinguishable from any other
shoreline along the 80-mile perimeter of Priest Lake.
Just so, if you want your 'bag of sand' to count,
to mean something, don't procrastinate the day
of your attention to the important details of
your life. Repair relationships, and build
consensus; nurture your appreciation
of family, and fortify the bonds
of love with those who matter
the most.

If, through willful neglect, carelessness, or inattention, the sixty-five feet of our beach at Northwinds were to be left unattended for only a few years, it would very quickly become indistinguishable from any other shoreline along the 80-mile perimeter of Priest Lake. Just so, if you want your 'bag of sand' to count, to mean something, don't postpone any longer turning your attention to the important details of our lives. Repair relationships, build consensus, and nurture your appreciation of our family. Fortifying the bonds of love with those who matter the most creates castles in the sand whose battlements pierce the sky and reach all the way to the gates of heavens.

The smallest bags of sand
that are sprinkled on our beach will
contribute to its solidarity, even though
it was built well above the summer pool level,
that it might be protected during the high water
accompanying the spring run-off. You might say:
"Yes, but each year Mother Nature wreaked havoc, and
I saw how hard you worked just to restore it to its former
condition, only to see the same thing recur the following
spring." It seemed like a never-ending battle that couldn't
be won. But that may have been Her point. Perhaps, She
intentionally gave me the power "to do", and each year,
when I responded to that call, I was intangibly added
upon in ways that would have been difficult to
duplicate, even if, in Her divine design, She
had blessed me with other talents and
different circumstances.

The grains of
sand that rest in the palm of
your hand represent just a tiny
fraction of that which has been spread
over our beach during the past quarter of a
century. Our contributions should prompt
us to ask ourselves if we think our efforts
will make a difference, and if so, can we
recognize and acknowledge the hand of
Divine Providence, and make sure
that it will continue to exert
a positive influence on
our behavior?"

Are those flecks of gold we see in
the bags of sand we are spreading on the
beach? Wrote the poet: "My life is but a weaving
between my Lord and me. I cannot choose the colors.
He worketh steadily. Oft times He weaveth sorrow, and
I, in foolish pride, forget He sees the upper, and I the under
side. Not 'til the loom is silent, and the shuttles cease to fly,
shall God unroll the canvas and explain the reason why. The
dark threads are as needful in the Weaver's skillful hand, as
the threads of gold and silver in the pattern He has planned."
I spent years hauling sand down to the beach, only to see
most of it wash away in storms, because as the poem
points out, "the dark threads are as needful in the
Weaver's skillful hand, as the threads of gold
and silver in the pattern He has
planned."

Anciently, the purity of gold
was tested with a smooth rock called
a touchstone. When the metal was rubbed
across the stone, it left a mark that could be
matched to a color on a chart. The higher the
percentage of gold, the more yellow would be
the mark. I am quite sure that, were we to
rub our beach sand (that has tickled
the toes of so many of our family
members) across a touchstone, a
distinctive yellow trail would
reveal the glint of gold.

I have always wanted to
design a T-shirt that proclaimed:
"Priest Lake: Established 8,000 B.C."
Maybe I should have crafted one that
read: "Northwinds Beach: Established
1996-2022" and punctuated it with
sparkling jewels to remind me of the
magic of our Father's Divine Design.
If our expanding energy is aligned
with His blueprint, and we carry
out His will, the inertia of the
universe will sustain our
own creative efforts.

I've been a dad for
over half a century, and a
grandpa for nearly a quarter of
a century. From that perspective, I've
learned that we all belong to eternity.
Long after these grains of sand have
been ground into dust by incessant
wave action, we'll still be a family,
enhanced by even more grains
that will have been added in
the coming years to our
generational
'beach'.

As
Omar
Khayyam
has comforted
me, so I reassure
you to "think not I
dread to see my spirit
fly thru the dark gates
of mortality. Death has
no terror if life has been
true. It is living ill that
makes us fear to die."
Our beach stands as
a testament that
we have lived
well.

Our beach at Northwinds comes to mind when we "think of stepping on shore, and finding it heaven! Of taking a hand, and finding it God's hand. Of breathing a new air, and finding it celestial air. Of feeling invigorated, and finding it immortality. Of passing from storm and tempest to the unbroken calm of God's Rest. Of waking up, and finding it Home."
(Anonymous).

Sound,
touch, sight, smell,
and taste have left indelible
stamps on the passport of life that
stands as a witness to our experiences
at Northwinds on Priest Lake. So many
times we sat on the beach as our brains became
powerful blenders whisking these sensations into
frothy virgin piña colatas of perception that became
our windows on the world. They were our own personal
concoctions, and the recipes were proprietary. It was our life
experiences that created the zesty signature specialty drinks
complete with little paper umbrellas that fortified us against
the rain that would inevitably fall on many of our parades.
We were delighted to find these libations topped with the
empirical equivalents of mouthwatering cherries (to
hold our interest,) and with whipped cream (that
kept us coming back to the kitchen counter,
asking for more, please!)

Since I always have believed that
Divine Providence was on my side, I never
viewed the setbacks I encountered during the
construction of our beach as stumbling blocks.
Every grain of sand, including those that you
now hold in your hand and are about to extend
as a contribution to our communal effort, and
as an offering to the gods, has the potential to
be magically transformed. They may become
the elements of stepping-stones that are built
upon a firm foundation. They might even
provide us with additional footing that
will enable us to reach out and
touch the stars.

The 'habitable
zone' within a stellar
system is not too close nor is
it too far away from its host star.
It's also called the 'Goldilocks zone',
which is the area of space surrounding
a star within which any orbiting planets
could harbor liquid water, and where their
atmospheres could be made up of gases that
would not boil away into space, but would
retain just the right balance to support life
as we know it. On our beach, we seek a
similar equilibrium, one that exists
between the wind and the waves,
and between the sand and the
jewels that hide among
its grains.

Currently, our beach consists of at least 100 yards of sand, or roughly 400 billion grains. How many stars are born per year in the known universe? Astrophysicists have arrived at a consensus: 400 billion stars. How have they calculated this number? Our galaxy produces 3 new stars per year, and 1 star per year 'dies.' So, 3-1 = 2. But to be on the safe side, let's say that the net gain is only 1 star per year, in our galaxy, and let's assume that our galaxy is 'typical' of all 400 billion galaxies in the universe. Therefore, the cumulative number of stars born every year is 400 billion. That's roughly 1.1 billion new stars per day, 456 million stars per hour, or almost 800,000 stars per minute, (about the length of time it will take to read this paragraph), or 12,684 stars per second. Think about that as you spend 30 seconds scattering your handful of sand, about 400,000 grains, on the beach. Truly, God is Great, and our beach becomes the humble prototype of worlds without end.

Job asked 2 questions to which I now have the good fortune to be given answers: "Canst thou find out God? Canst thou find out the Almighty?" His answer was one for the ages. In our day, we would say that it explored a frontier that bordered on the unknown possibilities of existence. God's habitation, he wrote, "is as high as heaven (and) the measure thereof is longer than the earth, and broader than the sea." (Job 11:7 & 9).

Maybe the real reason
why our beach at Northwinds has
always seemed like a "work in progress" has
been because it is not the destination, but rather
the journey, that is important. Maybe the sand on the
beaches of our lives is meant to be swept away from time
to time into unexplored oceans. Maybe we are allegorically
destined to be cast upon far shores to discover the unknown
possibilities of existence. "There is a tide (after all) which
taken at the flood, leads on to fortune. Omitted, all the
voyage of (our lives) is bound in shallows and in
miseries. On such a full sea are we now afloat,
and we must take the current when it
serves, or lose our ventures."
(Shakespeare).

Unlike the sand on our beach that, by nature, has been ground down to dust from the granite cirques within the Selkirk Mountains, every atom in our bodies came from the explosion of a star that had gone supernova, or perhaps, some scientists believe, from the cataclysmic collision of two neutron stars. The atoms in one hand probably came from a different star than those in the other. We are all stardust, but it wasn't created at the beginning of time. It was created in the nuclear furnaces of stars. The only way that it found its way into our bodies was because those stars were selfless enough to explode, and to scatter the seeds of life throughout the cosmos. By extension, this takes the Atonement to an almost incomprehensible level. In a sense that is both mystical and magical, both Jesus and the stars He created died so that we could be here today.

Each bag of sand that's
found its way to Northwinds
has contributed to a harmonic pulse
and the surge of a spiritual essence that
rhythmically beats thru all of nature. Its
currents wash upon our shores in a perfect
cadence with the cosmos. It circumscribes a
vast ocean of thought whose depth cannot
be plumbed, even though we often try to
compartmentalize it as the 'Creation'.
Think about that and sense its power
the next time you bend down and
scoop up a handful of sand. Feel
every grain as it runs down
between your fingers to
join its companions
on the beach.

Just
as the action of
wind and water has
transformed our beach over
the years, our mortal clay has
been molded by the Master with the
potter's rib of participation, the needle
tool of experience, the wire cutting device
of practice, the trimming loops of execution,
and the sponges of performance. His creativity
sparks delightful diversity stimulating both
invention and imagination. Every blazing
sunset we have savored at Northwinds and
each jewel we have discovered on its beach
reminds us that we carry out our lives
in Technicolor, and not in the drab
monotones of ennui, thanks to
the creative influence of our
Heavenly Father.

From our
beach, we lift our
eyes to the heavens and
to the swath of light from our
galaxy. We remember that myths
and traditions from around the world
and from the dim recesses of memory have
given the Milky Way its name and explained
its origin. The Greeks believed it was created when
suckling Heracles dribbled the breast milk of Hera,
the wife of Zeus, across the evening sky. It was also
described as the trail to Mount Olympus, the home of
the Gods, and as the path of ruin made by the chariot
of the Sun God Helios. In Sanskrit, the Milky Way
was called Akash Ganga, or Ganges of the Heavens,
and was thought to be sacred. Hindu cosmology
describes the galaxy as an ocean of milk that
was churned by the gods for a thousand
years, to release Amrita, the nectar
of immortal life. For those of us
in the modern age, the Milky
Way simply marks the
path to the celestial
city of God.

Each time
one of our little ones
ecstatically finds a jewel on the
beach, imagine as well the thrill that
I now have of finally discovering the castle
of enchantment behind the hills of time, and to
have found that growing 'older' at the rate of one day
every twenty-four hours had been strictly and uniquely a
quality of mortality and a brilliant mechanism designed to
afford me an opportunity to gauge the approach of my reunion
with God in the eternal world. I have learned that I lived my
life in only one dimly lighted corner of reality, but now,
I "flourish in immortal youth, unhurt amidst the war
of elements, the wreck of matter, and the crash
of worlds." (Joseph Addison).

Find
somewhere
to spread a bag
of sand, and create
a special place to set a
chair or lay out a blanket,
that you might not only
find rest, but also feel
beneath your feet the
solidarity of our
family.

Predictions about the world's end have come true! For some of us, the veil that had been drawn across our minds has been erased, and time is no more as we ease into eternity. We lucky few have reconciled to the native and more natural environment of our former home. The lion lies down with the lamb, and eats straw, and no-one comes to hurt in all the holy mountain of the Lord. The waters have been calmed and the north storms that once ravaged the beaches of our lives are no more. As we gaze out across the wide expanse of eternity, we discover that the summer pool level of the lake has been stabilized, and it is as a sea of glass, revealing the sparkle of countless thousands of Jewels that festoon its shoreline. Our eyes are touched by the angels so that we may see things as they really are, and behold for the first time the work of God's hands.

Mother Nature has
exhorted us to drink copiously
and unceasingly from a fountain
of truth, that we might slake our thirst
for principles that stabilize our lives and
gyroscopically orient us toward heaven. The
bedrock beneath our beach furnishes a footing
to appreciate the ocean of life. It blesses us with
stability in an uncertain world and balances
our lives by giving us tools to make course
corrections. By exercising faith in God,
we are given plot points and power to
move from safety on the shoreline
of sand. We confidently venture
into the unknown, with Him
beside us, as we navigate
treacherous waters.

If we ever hope to be able to
fathom the mystery of mysteries and to
be at peace with our place in the cosmos, we must
do more than just scatter a few bags of sand or gather
the jewels on our beach. We must read, fear, hope, and pray.
We must lift the latch and force the way, as Sir Walter Scott
suggested. We must expend soul sweat, and our inspiration must
be preceded by perspiration, because our enlightenment, in order to
be meaningful, must be deserved. It must be earned line upon line,
and precept upon precept, only after payment with the equity of
exercise. It cannot come freely to those who wander the cosmos,
who are tossed to and fro by every wind of doctrine because
they lack the discipline to unlock the power thru which
The Plan of Salvation promises to bless all of the
teachable children of our Father in Heaven.

Those of us who have
felt the warmth of the sand on our
beach at Northwinds, and who with their
toes have traced the course of constellations
in its grains, who have felt the wind beneath
their wings, know well the emotions expressed by
Ptolemy, who two millennia ago wrote: "When
I draw the paths of heavenly bodies, I no
longer touch the earth with my feet. I
stand in the presence of Zeus
himself, and take my
fill of ambrosia."

Scatter a bagful of jewels
across our beach in a celebratory
acknowledgement that I have come unto
Christ with shouts of acclamation, and
know that He has taken me Home, and
that joy fills my heart. I shall bow in
humble adoration, and with the
angels in heaven, I will add
my voice to proclaim: "My
God, how great Thou
art!"

We are all puzzles in various
stages of completion whose pieces define us.
They have been fashioned within the cauldron
of experience and express unique characteristics.
Our histories are works in progress, and not all
the chapters in the books of our lives have been
written. We are the stanzas in unfinished
symphonies and, like our beach, we are
continually evolving in an
eternal progression.

Trans-warp
drive, spore drive, subspace,
coaxial space, or even travel at the
speed of thought will not bring us any
closer to God than will simply preserving
in an unspoiled condition the beaches of our
lives. Our careful examination will reveal that
they have been seeded with a sparkling array of
jewels. It is our righteous stewardship, and not
the quantum slipstream drive or the omega
particle, that will bless us with the means
to draw upon the ultimate power source
in the universe, that stems from
our Divine Center.

Ashes and dust are both the literal
and figurative bookends of our lives.
How ironic, that we have emerged from
the drift of stars, and have evolved to the
point where we can sit on our beach and
contemplate the cosmos, and that in
the end, when we return Home, we
will immediately recognize the
familiar surroundings of
our premortal celestial
environment.

When
Ralph Waldo Emerson
declared: "Hitch your wagon
to a star", he knew that when we
bind our fortunes to the heavens,
we break free from normal temporal
constraints. The jewels we find on our
beach are of every color and hue, created
when their elements had been subjected
to temperature or pressure. Conversely,
when we're gliding effortlessly thru
life, we can be pretty sure that we're
going downhill. It seems that, in
order to make progress in the
construction of the beaches
of our lives, we all need
a healthy dose of
opposition.

It can be both
humbling and character
building to probe the dimensions
of our beach, let alone the far reaches of
heaven. Those who have tended our flowers,
raked our sand, and discovered the jewels that
are hidden beneath it, are the ticketed passengers of
Spaceship Earth, which is a modest and unassuming
vessel that is negotiating a vast cosmic ocean. The cost
of our vouchers won't be redeemed until we have reached
eternity, due to Jesus Christ's Atonement. Our Captain
only asks us to follow His Chart and to acknowledge
His proven navigational skills. During our journey,
His enlightened approach to education gives those
of us who are eager to learn from our mistakes
the freedom to make individual course
corrections without suffering from
irreparable consequences that
would be eternally
damaging.

Just as there
are myriad iterations of
jewels on our beach, one could
make the argument that diversity
in God's cosmos builds strength, while
uniformity and conformity weaken the
adaptive capacity of species. Pliancy that
is the result of diversity encourages His
creations to continually transform into
new and refreshing expressions. It may
seem counterintuitive, but diversity
in both the jewels on our beach and
in those who delight in finding
them is a principle that has
been intertwined with
progression.

"Meet Joe Black"
was a film that was loosely based
on the 1934 motion picture "Death Takes
a Holiday." At its conclusion, the protagonist,
who is about to die, asks Death: "Should I be afraid?"
When Death gently answers him and says: "Not a man
like you," we know that, in the face of the inevitable,
everything will be okay. If we have lived by faith,
when it's our time to let go, and to reach out to
touch the stars, we, too, will sense the warm
embrace of heaven and find that God
has blessed us with an equally
powerful reassurance
of peace.

When we gaze up at the
night sky, we are looking back in
time. The light arriving at our retinas
from the farthest objects in the Milky Way
has been zipping across the cosmos for tens of
thousands of years. We see its stars not as they
really are, but only as they were long ago. And yet,
when we shift our focus to investigate the eternities,
we witness the future. There must needs be opposition
for us to see things, not as they once were, or as they
now are, but as they may be. In a sense, we need
the opposition of death to really experience life,
and that everlastingly. We need the jewels
that are scattered about on the beaches
of our lives, though they may be
nothing more than colored
glass, to see that there
are diamonds in
the sky.

From our beach, we look up at the same stars as did Hawkeye, during the French & Indian Wars. We remember that he told Cora Munro: "At the birth of the Sun and of his brother the Moon, their mother died. So, the Sun gave to the Earth her body, from which was to spring all life. And he drew forth from her breast the stars, and these he threw into the night sky to remind him of her soul."
(James Fenimore Cooper, "The Last of The Mohicans").

We hope to be
blessed to dance
with the stars, both
in the cosmos and in
the heavens, as well as
on our beach. With the
pixie dust of sand and
gemstones settling on
our shoulders, we will
fly as if on wings of
eagles all the way to
the familiar abode
that we will share
with the angels
for eternity.

When God deigns to
reveal Himself within the
reality of our corruptible mortal
world and unveils the cosmos so that
His glory fills our beach, its elements
will melt like snow in the fervent heat
of the unrestrained Spirit. Under those
special circumstances, the mountains
will flow as rivers as they do during
the spring run-off, valleys will be
exalted, and rough places will be
made smooth, as has been the
case when, to make walking
more enjoyable, I've spread
gravel over the fractured
granite of the bed of
the lake, in our
swimming
area.

Each time
we feel the sand
beneath our feet, or
discover a jewel on the
beach, or gaze up at the
cosmos, a sense of awe
penetrutes to our core,
and we feel honored
to be the witnesses,
one more time, of
God's awesome
Creations.

Without
the discipline
of the Gospel to keep
our eyes focused on both
jewels and sandy beaches,
we will find ourselves locked
on telestial targets and will be
unable to see the forest for the trees.
We will look at the Milky Way and
catalogue its stars, but forget to count
our blessings. We will allow ourselves to
be governed by a rev-limiter on the power
plant that fuels not only light bulbs but
also galaxies and the heavens. We will be
drawn to the light like moths are to fire,
and will flutter around without purpose
until it becomes everlastingly too late
to make substantive change. Higher
level thinking will forever remain
just beyond the reach of our
comprehension.

If, from our beach, you were to pick up just 1 individual grain of sand and hold it up at arm's length against the night sky, hidden behind the blocked-out area would be 2,000 galaxies, each of which contains 100 billion to 1 trillion or more stars.

Spiritual
enlightenment can
create a celestial bridge
that transports us past the
improbabilities of life to the
stability of understanding,
not only of this world that is
represented by our beach and
its jewels, but also by eternal
realms that lie just beyond
the horizon, and that are
evidenced by fire in
the sky.

Add a bag of sand
to our beach, that it might
be better suited to become our
jumping off point on a voyage to
the stars. Perhaps we'll join intrepid
explorers such as Captain James Cook,
who wrote in his journal: "I intend to
go not only farther than anyone
has been before me, but as far
as I think it is possible
for anyone to go."

The jewels that sparkle in the
sunlight on the beaches of our lives
gently validate a spiritual certainty:
Heavenly light permeates the cosmos. We
feel the infusion of its power, and our own
enlightenment is confirmed by an inner
yearning to be at one with the Infinite.
This feeling is intangible, and it is
Indescribable. It is inarticulate,
and yet from within the core
of our being it quietly
speaks peace to our
souls.

On our
beach at the
eventide, we are
poised at the edge of
forever, ready to push
off onto journeys that
will curry us to the fur
reaches of a vast cosmic
sea. We are enlightened
explorers who have been
given fire for the deed
by the Holy Spirit
of God.

The jewels that
we've scattered across
our beach publish for all to
see the proclamation that we
are the offspring of Deity. If we
look closely, in their facets we
will find the reflection of His
majesty, for we are His
doppelgangers.

If,
today, you
think to defer until
tomorrow morning your
commission to scatter your
bag of sand, by the time you
wake up after a refreshing eight
hours of sleep, (that is eight hours
of active labor in the birthing center
of the universe), 547,945,205 stars
will have been born. That's over half
a billion stars, equivalent to one and
a half billion new 'suns' every day,
for as long as time exists. God
must have His reasons for
orchestrating such a
light show.

We scatter handfuls of jewels across our
beach, and their sparkle catches the attention of
our little ones. We hope that they are learning how
special it is to walk in the light, as it shows them the
way. However, we trust that they will learn another
principle, as well: That darkness is as needful
as daylight, since it is only during the
night that God can reveal to us the
breathtaking majesty of
His stars in the
Heavens.

Our beach has
taught us valuable lessons
about balance. When we take
to heart principles that reinforce
equilibrium, our faith is kindled,
our testimonies are protected, and
ultimately, our souls are saved.
We better understand how we
fit in to the grand divine
design of God's
cosmos.

Alma explained to Corianton: "All is as one day with God, and time only is measured unto men." (Alma 40:8) Einstein was probably right and time may be relative. However, that doesn't give us a free pass to postpone our obligation to scatter jewels across the beaches of our lives. We need to do it, do it right, and do it right now.

Those of us who have been
given the blessing to run on ahead will
awaken to a greater vision that is blinding at
first. But as our eyes adjust to the light, perhaps
for the very first time we will be surprised to see the
world as it really was. We will begin to feel the creative
expression of powers that had always been within us and
will recognize them as the intrinsic energy that sought to
bring us closer to heaven. In the end, we will realize that we
have not been alone in the universe, and more than that, we
will discover that God's divine potential has been ignited
within us. Our new perspective will broaden as do ripples
radiating outward from rocks thrown into the still
waters of our perceptual ponds. Our cascade of
questions may be simple, but within the
answers, if we listen carefully, we
will be able to hear what God is
thinking.

If our Northwinds
beach were to be depleted of
sand through our own neglect,
or if we never bothered to maintain
the supply of jewels hidden among
its grains, or if our weathered wine
barrels were never replenished with
fresh flowers, we would certainly
be found wanting at the day of
reckoning when contact will
be firmly re-established
with the Spirit.

If we only casually
observe the jewels on our beach
as if there were nothing beyond their
outward appearance that should command
our attention, or when we examine ourselves,
our persona, integrity, devotions, and loyalties
with a myopic view, it will be the same old story,
even though our insipid inspections are conducted
from opposite directions. Even if we do both, our
cumulative comprehension will barely scratch
the surface of the magnificent creations of
God, while contributing very little to the
understanding of our relationship
with the depths of eternity that
define His holy habitation.

We must look at the sand and
the jewels on the beaches of our lives
differently than we have in the past, with a
greater appreciation of our similarities, and a
more tolerant view of our differences, because "we
are all connected to each other biologically, to the
earth chemically, and to the rest of the universe
atomically." (Neil deGrasse Tyson). "The
cosmos is within us, and we are made
of star-stuff. Collectively, we are a
way for the universe to know
itself." (Carl Sagan).

If the sand
from the beaches of
our lives gets fouled in our
gears, poorly managed friction
will heat us up and wear us out. Of
course, we do not want to glide smoothly
and effortlessly thru life, because that often
means we are going downhill. In contrast, as we
steadily move upward to new heights of achievement,
encountering and overcoming opposition along the way,
we'll find ourselves headed in the direction of the stars in
the heavens. Thru resistance training, our muscle mass
will increase, enabling us to bear heavier loads of jewels,
to run on our beaches without becoming weary, and
to walk beside the firepits of our lives without
fainting, no matter how daunting our
challenges may seem.

God
Invites each of
us to hang on for
dear life as we follow
Him along a trajectory
that will take us from the
launch platform of our beach
all the way to the farthest reaches
of His creations. The countdown to
liftoff has already begun, and it has
been punctuated by the verb 'to come'.
If we choose to obey Him, exactly where,
when, and how far He will lead us has
been established only by our faith.
All we can say with any degree
of certainty is that it will
be out of this world!

There is an
enchantment that betrays
our fascination with the jewels that
decorate our beach. It can be discovered in our
appreciation of the faintest afterglow that hints of
celestial glory. For those of us who believe, its serves as
a beacon that will unerringly guide us past the reefs upon
which we might otherwise founder as we navigate the creations
of God. Even though we may have commenced our journey of
self-discovery from the farthest spiritual, emotional, and
intellectual reaches of a vast and turbulent galactic
ocean, its light will be powerful enough to expose
Satan's shoals as it leads us out of danger
toward the safe harbor of the Gospel.

As you sprinkle handfuls of sand on our beach, (hopefully, with the Milky Way out in full force!) so could it be said of one who has died, and whose dust has returned to the earth: "Here lies a child from a distant star, but the soil is not foreign to him, for in death he returns to the universe."
(Anonymous).

Shakespeare said that all the world's
a stage, but what better setting could have
been created to enact the story of our lives than at
Northwinds? For many, it has been a venue for their
opening scenes, and for others, the location of their final
curtain call. As the eyes of our understanding are opened,
we discover that, although we can't start over and write new
beginnings to the scripts that describe our lives, we can begin
now to create new endings. Priest Lake holds us firmly in its
grasp, and the only explanation is that our lives must be
fairy tales that are being written by the finger of God.
We are unprofitable understudies, who will forever
remain in the debt of the Creative Force behind
the Greatest Story Ever Told.

Spread a bagful of sand on our beach, and you will have a firm foundation when you look up at the stars. You will be able to discern the "fire-folk sitting in the air in bright boroughs and circled citadels." (Gerald Hopkins, "The Starlight Night").

Perhaps God created
the Milky Way to illuminate
the pathway to enlightenment with
a trail of star-studded jewels high above
our beach. It will lead to broad boulevards
lined with fig trees that are laden with
fruit, flooded with a celestial glow,
caressed by a soothing breeze,
and paved in cobblestones
that glint of gold.

"Great
Spirit, Maker of
all life. A warrior goes
to you swift and straight
as an arrow shot into the Sun.
Welcome him as he takes his place
at the council fire of my people. He
is Uncas, my son. Tell them to be
patient and ask death for speed.
For they are all there but one; I
Chingachgook - Last of the
Mohicans." One day, we
will all take our places
around the council
fires of our
people.

In the same
spirit that drives us to search
for jewels scattered on our beach (some
of which might mark the nighttime trails
left by Woodland Elves), Peter Pan revealed
to Wendy that she could find Neverland
by taking the second star to the right
and continuing straight on
'til morning.

Pushing midnight
in the middle of summer,
we have seen "evening make its
quiet entrance across the skies, out
thru the darkness that, quivering, dies,
while the Milky Way, "beautiful, broad,
and white, is fashioned of "silver rays
and stolen out of the ruins of day."
We watch in wonder as its pale
bridge grows, "built by the
Architect of night."
(Anon).

In many of the Hollywood portrayals with which we are familiar, extra-terrestrial encounters are accompanied by blinding light. We don't know if that will be the case when we make first contact with heaven, but in our mind's eye, we have set the stage for a dazzling 'close encounter' by strewing a cascade of glittering jewels across our beach. In the first kind, an unidentified person or object is seen, but without environmental interaction. In the second kind, there are observable physical effects. In a close encounter of the third kind, however, extra-terrestrial beings make tangible first contact with humans. It is this last scenario that paints a portrait of Him Whose identity is intertwined with light. We look forward to the day when, punctuated by diamonds and other gemstones, we shall see the Savior "coming in the clouds with great power and glory." (Mark 13:26).

Each handful of sand that
is added to our beach contributes to
a stable platform upon which we can broaden
our perspective, expand our depth of field, and lift
our eyes to strain beyond the limited horizon of our
vision. The solid foundation beneath our feet will allow
us to be cast off into the stream of a revelatory expansion
of knowledge. Protected from the influence of the raging
storms that so frequently come barreling down out of
the north, we will instead be carried along in the
quickening currents of direct experience
with the heavens.

The jewels
that we cast upon
our beach sparkle with
a light that reaches "unto
the midst of heaven" itself.
(Deuteronomy 4:11). If we
follow its luminescent
trail, we just might
witness a brilliant
conduit opening
into the cosmos,
to reveal the
household
of God.

Countless times, on moonless
nights, we have lingered on our beach to dream
with the mystics who see "torrents of light and rivers
of the air, along whose bed the glimmering stars are seen
like gold and silver sands in some ravine, where mountain
streams have left their channels bare." We have witnessed our
Heavenly Father "descend in the sheen of His celestial armor,
on serene and quiet nights, when all the heavens are fair,"
and we have marveled at the stardust that is evidence
of a divine Presence, as it has "whirled aloft and
flown from the invisible chariot wheels of
God." (William Wordsworth,
"The Galaxy").

The
jewels
upon our
beach that
so radiantly
sparkle with a
thousand facets
poignantly teach
us that there is no
darkness so dense,
so menacing, or so
forbidding, that it
is impenetrable
to light.

On evenings too frequent to count,
an hour or so after sunset, we have sat on our
beach and gazed up at the darkening sky, allowing
ourselves to be captivated by the twinkling evidence of the
Celestial City of God, as it has been unfolded to our view. On
many such occasions, we have been unconsciously compelled to
silently recite the familiar words of what could be described as the
first audible 'prayer' of many of God's children: "Star light, star
bright, the first star I see tonight. I wish I may, I wish I might,
have the wish I wish tonight." Our petitions are still as fresh
and as optimistic as the day they were first delivered, and
we remain eternally hopeful that they will find their way
to God's listening ear. I have now returned Home, to live
with Him forever, and the wish I grant to you from
the first star you see tonight is that you will
embrace my testimony that He hears
and answer our prayers.

An illuminated pathway glitters with
fairy stones as it leads to our beach. It invites us to
take the second star to the right and go straight on 'til
morning. That formula allows us to "be like the birds, that
pausing in their flight a while on boughs to light, feel them
give way beneath their feet, and yet sing, knowing that they
have wings." (Victor Hugo). We will go where only eagles
have dared to fly, and we will ascend to the heavens, to
a celestial rendezvous with God. Surrounded by a
host of angels, from blazing glory He will
extend to us an invitation to embrace
our divine destiny.

Even
our hesitant
efforts to extend
our vision beyond the
furthest horizons will be
rewarded by God's assurance
that when our eyes are single to His
glory, our "whole bodies shall be filled
with light, and there shall be no darkness
in (us), and that body which is filled with
light comprehendeth all things." (D&C 88:67).
The jewels on our beach testify of the Master of
the Universe and the Creator of Worlds Who
has provided a talisman of gemstones
to protect us and to heal us of
our wounds.

"O Lord my God,
when I in awesome wonder
consider all the worlds Thy Hands
have made, I see the stars, I hear the rolling
thunder, Thy power throughout the universe
displayed." ("How Great Thou Art"). On the one
hand, these evidences of God make our little beach
seem insignificant, but on the other, they validate
the certainty that we can find a little bit of heaven
just about anywhere, and especially if we look
all around us from the unique perspective
that has been afforded by the blessing
we have been given to experience
what life has to offer, from
Northwinds.

Take some
of the sand from
your baggie and let it fall
thru your fingers, and feel the
smooth surfaces of the jewels as you
toss them here and there. But know that
heaven is our natural element. It is the ether
that even now fills our lungs and invigorates us
with celestial air, and it is the state of being that we all
intuitively call our Home. God created the physical world,
and established governing laws that were designed to lead
us back into His presence. Because we are spiritual beings
having mortal experiences, we sometimes feel that we are
not synchronized with our environment. If that is so,
our greatness and power will only be manifest when
"the stars fade away, the sun himself grow dim
with age, and nature sink in years." Then,
we "shall flourish in immortal youth,
unhurt amidst the war of elements,
the wreck of matter, and the
crash of worlds." (Joseph
Addison).

Even
tho I've carried
yards and yards of
sand to beautify our
beach and make it more
comfortable to move about
the shoreline at Northwinds,
and despite the contribution of
your baggie to its stability and
sense of permanency, if we will
look up at the stars instead of
down at our feet, it will be
a lot easier to see where
we're going.

Arching high above our beach
at Northwinds lies the magnificent
sweep of the Milky Way. As we inhale its
aether, the Spirit quietly whispers to us that
comfortably nestled among its stars "dwell the
spirits of the blessed, clothed in radiance. It is a
habitation that has been marvelously planned
by God for (us) to occupy in love and rest."
(Wordsworth, "The Stars are Mansions
Built by Nature's Hand").

"The past, the present, and the future exist as one." (Harriet Beecher Stowe). They breathe together. Time and space, our reality, are the final frontiers. We all push off from the beaches of our lives, some sooner than others, as we continue our personally tailored adventures whose design is divine. The passenger manifests have already recorded each of our names, and angels are waiting to check the list twice. Our travel itineraries include the exploration of strange new worlds where we will seek out new life and new civilizations, and we are excited to boldly go where no mortal has gone before, for it is eternity that is the final stop of our train that is bound for glory.

On their journey to our beach
at Northwinds, photons from the most
distant celestial objects in the cosmos have
traveled thru the vacuum of space at a constant
velocity of 5.8 trillion miles per year. That's 5.8
thousand billion miles each year for 13.8 billion
years. To put things in perspective, as we gaze at
the heavens from our dock, starlight that is just
now reaching our eyes was only 23,200 trillion
miles from Earth just 4,000 years ago. In that
distant past, our ancestors who lived on the
shore of Priest Lake were still knapping
arrowheads out of obsidian, so we
haven't been players on the
universal stage for
very long.

You may not know that the
lights that appear in the night
sky are actually tiny holes that
have been poked thru heaven's floor
by playful angels. In a sense, we act
in a similar way. Each time we scatter
jewels across our beach, if we toss them
high enough, we are, in fact, shooting
for the moon. And yet, if we miss our
mark, all isn't necessarily lost. With
enough power behind our efforts, we
could be drawn to the angels' stars.
We might even find ourselves in
the midst of that mischievous
heavenly host, and come to
appreciate more fully
God's sense of
humor!

When
we look very
closely at the jewels
that adorn our beach,
we will discover in every
multi-faceted reflection the
countenance of a star child,
for we were created in the
image and likeness
of God.

As we look out across the
quiet waters of the lake, we are
mesmerized beneath an evening
sky that steals our imaginations.
The stars in the heavens are wrapped
in a fiery red blanket of clouds that
merges as one with the sand on our
beach. In the whispering wind, we
can distinctly hear the voice of
God reassuring us that our
world is brimming over
with possibilities that
are unlimited.

For now, we
walk across our beach
with a sharp eye, looking
for the occasional hidden jewel.
But we can only concentrate on one
gemstone at a time. As Georgia Byng
observed: "There's no time like the present
and no present like time and life can be over
in the space of a rhyme." In our future state,
we will see from multiple perspectives, set free
from the myopic vision that currently limits
our sight to specific objects of our attention in
the physical and temporal present. As Albert
Einstein declared after the passing of an old
friend: "This death signifies nothing. For
us believing physicists, the distinction
between past, present, and future is
only an illusion, even if it is
a stubborn one."

The principles that
distinguish the Great Plan of
The Eternal God do not allow us to
predict the future by simply plotting the
position of the stars that wheel with celestial
precision across the night sky. (Of course,
the scriptures teach us that it is the earth
rotating on its axis, rather than heaven,
that moves.) But still, we are able to
chart the coordinates of our eternal
progress every time we witness
the ethereal light that dances
about the glittering jewels
that have been deposited
by God to define the
boundaries of the
beaches of our
lives.

I've put countless yards
of sand on our beach, and I know
that your contributions to that effort
will continue to be significant. Always
look for ways that you can make a
difference, no matter how small
they may seem to be
at the time.

It has been within the
peaceful borders of our sandy
beach that we have discovered the tools
of perspective and context, that we might
better understand our environment, while
its terrestrial jewels that are scattered about
provide counterpoint for clarity. It is light
and truth that endow us with the ability
to 'see' the spiritual world within which
we are enveloped. These include many
celestial glories and wonders in the
heavens that cannot be discerned
until the finger of God has
touched our mortal
eyes.

Jehovah stood
In the presence of our Father
prior to the creation of Northwinds.
From within His royal pavilion, we can
almost hear Him declare: "We will go down,
for there is sand there, and we will take of these
materials, and we will make a beach." (Abraham
3:24). All that was necessary was for the Lord to
go 'down' and establish, or set in motion, all of
the laws, bounds, and conditions by which our
beach could take shape in its lovely setting
in Idaho's Panhandle, at Priest Lake,
just North of the Narrows.

Notwithstanding our
confidence that we will be
blessed with visions of glory, our
family, like so many others, needs to
double-down, that, as it mourns the loss
of departed loved ones, it might not lose the
eternal perspective of the ebb and flow of life
upon the vast ocean of thought that exists not
only upon our beach, but also throughout the
cosmos. Stretching our minds and spirits
thru faith "speaks volumes of happiness,
of joy, and of gratitude to the soul.
Thank the Lord he has revealed
these principles to us."
(Joseph Smith).

During the dog
days of summer that we
have spent on our beach, (July
3 to August 11), we have learned to
appreciate its natural environment that
is so vibrantly real. As we have looked north
to the sun-dappled outlines of Green Bonnet,
Mollies' and Phoebe's Tips, and Trapper Peak,
we have been reminded that we mustn't allow
ourselves to be strangled by the illusions of
reality, or by the profane baubles of the
world whose opacity obstructs our
ability to see what is really
out there.

Our
beach,
in concert
with Its jewels
of every imaginable
color, is only a shadow
of things to come, thut we
cannot expect to understand
at the level of comprehension of
our Father in Heaven. For, now, as
Paul did: "We see through a glass,
darkly, but then face to face. Now
(we) know in part; but then shall
(we) know even as also (we) are
known." (1 Corinthians
13:12).

Upon our beach, there has always been room and to spare for Greeks and Romans, Jews and Gentiles, and Nephites and Lamanites, the rich as well as the poor, and for those who might be black or white, and bond or free. Thanks to the Atonement, there have been places under our red umbrellas for both Venusians and Martians, believers and infidels, and for saints and sinners, as well as for our Golden Retrievers Katie, Danner, and Mackensie, (although they have really preferred lying under our zero gravity chairs.)

In a coming day,
when it has been fine-tuned
to a sanctified state, our beach
"will be made like unto" the jewels
that adorn it, "and will be a Urim and
Thummim to the inhabitants who dwell
thereon, whereby all things pertaining to
an inferior beach, or all beaches of a lower
order, will be made manifest to those who
dwell on it." (See D&C 130:9). Across its
broad expanse of sand, there will forever
be one department after another, "and
so on to an eternal progression, not
only of our shoreline, but also in
exaltation and eternal lives."
(Brigham Young).

We resort to the utilization of
abstractions in our own feeble attempts to describe
God. Thoughts cannot be shaped, nor words formed, nor
sentences framed, to accurately convey His glory. Figures of
speech are used because we would otherwise be at a complete loss for
words, when grasping for even a basic description of His profoundly
metaphysical reality. To Moses, the presence of the Lord appeared as "a
flame of fire out of the midst of a bush: and he looked, and behold, the
bush burned with fire, and the bush was not consumed." (Exodus
3:2). At Northwinds, we might say, as did another of Heavenly
Father's children who witnessed, as we have on many occasions,
His signature Aurora: "We beheld a circle of green, blue, and
orange swirling thru the night sky like a ballroom dancer
performing a waltz. It was flowing with such grace
that we were speechless, and remained entranced
for a quarter hour and more."

As we break free from
our limiting beliefs, the power
of our potential will be unleashed
Daniel Burnham opined that as we sit
upon the beaches of our lives, we should
"make no small plans, for they have not
the power to stir our souls." At the end of
the day, we will find the broad expanse
of our galaxy full of magical things
that are the interstellar equivalents
of the superb jewels on our beach.
These are patiently waiting for
our wits to grow sharper,
to better appreciate
them.

On the
shore of Priest
Lake, our building of
the North Idaho equivalent
of Camelot has been a work in
progress permitting us to be self-
directed, self-managed, self-propelled,
and self-motivated, while augmenting
our sense of self-esteem and self-worth.
We've never been so focused on ourselves,
however, that we were tempted to dismiss
the divine design of the Architect of the
cosmos, Whose hand has guided, not
only the creation and evolution of
our beach, its preservation and
its prosperity, but also (and
far more importantly,)
the trajectory of
our lives.

The day is coming when
our mortal must put on immortality,
and our bodies which moulder in corruption will
become incorruptible. (See Mormon 6:21). This will
be accomplished when our Father in Heaven carries us
into the greater light of His Celestial Kingdom of
glory, a feat that may be represented by the
contrast between the coarse sand and
the brilliant jewels that exist in
harmony on our beach
at Priest Lake.

Brigham Young asked: "When you lay down
this tabernacle, where are you going? Into the spiritual
world. Where is the spirit world? It is right here. Do the spirits
go beyond the boundaries of the organized earth? No, they do not.
They can see us, but we cannot see them unless our eyes are opened."
It may just be that we have been receiving assistance from the unseen
world, and have not been alone in our efforts to keep our beach well
supplied with jewels. Perhaps, there are 'Woodland Elves', after
all, who are the real custodians of the treasury that keeps the
sand decorated with the glittering baubles that draw the
rapt attention of our little ones who are delighted by
discovery. Maybe their occasional sightings of
the shy and elusive elves are real, and it is
we, the grownups, who only need to
believe, in order to see.

Priest Lake teaches
us again and again that we are
negotiating turbulent waters. It is here
that we learn that only the ablest mariners can
focus their nautical skills and trim their sails to set
a course that will lead them unerringly back to our dock
at Northwinds. The same storms that might cause others to
founder, fills the sails of the vessels whose captains are capable
navigators. They may not see the boulders that define our beach
and mark their destination, for it may be over the horizon. At
times, the tack of the vessel may appear to be taking their
ship of state away from our line of red umbrellas and
chairs. But if correct principle are followed, as the
day follows night, the safety and security of
landfall at Northwinds will be sure.

The Milky Way
that arches above our
heads on moonless nights is
"a broad and ample road whose dust
is gold." (John Milton, "Paradise Lost").
Sometimes, gravitational forces cause that
dust to coalesce into stars or planets, and
at other times, it simply undergoes a
transformation to become the
jewels that we find on
our beach.

It seems as if it were only yesterday that I shouldered bags of sand to the beach, from a staging area up on the driveway. Now you will continue that effort beginning with the contribution of your own baggie. One day, you will discover, as I have, that time flies like an arrow, and fruit flies like ripe bananas.

The abundance of jewels on
our beach is maintained by the zealous efforts
of those elusive Woodland Elves whose motivation
comes from a spiritual propellant that is out of this
world. By comparison, the Space Shuttle burned
835,958 gallons of terrestrial fuel to put itself
in orbit. $1,380,000.00 was required to pay
that gas bill, each time she flew. That's
$1.38 million more than the cost of
the Elves' program, which is free,
by the way, and requires of
us nothing more than
an expenditure
of faith.

In a coming day, we may be
surprised to discover that ever since the
moment of Creation, there have stubbornly
persisted certain locations in space and time that
even now are "without form, and void," to the end that
there continues to be "darkness" here and there, then and
now, upon the face of the deep." (Genesis 1:2). Perhaps, in
these places, worlds and lives abound while improvement
and progression have one eternal round. Beyond the
reaches of our beach and outside the boundaries of
observation, there may be no end to matter,
space, spirit, or race. (See: William W.
Phelps, "If You Could Hie
to Kolob").

The tranquility of the cosmos
can be disrupted by the introduction
of the voice of the Lord from eternal worlds.
At Northwinds, we sometimes hear it as the roar
of thunder rolling out of the Upper Priest Lake basin.
We witness the manifestation of lightning as a rift, or
a tear, in the very fabric of spacetime. and as a dramatic
disturbance in the order of nature. If we listen carefully,
and in particular, if we allow ourselves to be enraptured
by these exhibitions, we can hear thru the tumult the
voice of God as it speaks "marvelous words which
cannot be uttered." (Helaman 5:33).

Perhaps
there are so
many jewels on
our beach and stars
in the sky because we
need special twinkling
objects of our attention to
wish upon. Sometimes, it's
better to lower our eyes as we
seek out answers, but mostly
we should look up and follow
that second star on the left,
then continue strait on 'til
morning. Life should be
a journey that carries
us in the direction
of our dreams.

From
the unreserved
seating section on
our beach, we behold "a
glorious dawn. It is not a
sunrise, but a galaxy-rise;
a morning filled with 400
billion suns; the rising
of the Milky Way!"
(Carl Sagan).

In a tender expression of her love for the young Montague, Juliet says of Romeo: "When he shall die, take him and cut him up in little stars, and he will make the face of heaven so fine that all the world will be in love with night, and pay no worship to the garish sun." (Shakespeare).

In The Old Testament book of the same name, it is recorded that the prophet Jeremiah saw the Earth as it was before the forces of nature had been applied to terrestrial objects. He described the tumultuous conditions that unfolded before his eyes, as if they were the elements of a breathtaking panorama. The land "was without form, and void; and the heavens had no light. (Then, he) beheld the mountains, and, lo, they trembled, and all the hills moved." (Jeremiah 4:23). Even the jewels that would one day garnish our beach at Northwinds had not yet been quickened to reveal their native luster, but were dull and lifeless.

At Priest Lake, some of us have had experiences similar to that of Elijah, who conversed with the Lord Jehovah. As he did, "a great and strong wind rent the mountains, and brake in pieces the rocks before the Lord ... and after(wards) a fire." (1 Kings 19:11-12). The Lord's Presence was manifest as these most dramatic forces in nature. We witness similar signs at Northwinds. Since His Second Coming will be equally powerful, the outlook doesn't look very good for the longevity of our beach. And yet, we know that when The Mount of Olives is rent in twain, it will be a sign that our beach, and our firepit area, and even our horseshoe pit, will come together as they were in the days before Peleg.

It was
ordained in heaven
before the world was made
that we would grow comfortable
with the doctrine of individuality
as we exercise our free will. And yet,
as we do so, we feel the powerful exertion
of an equalizing influence. Ultimately,
we will find that, across the cosmos, "all
are alike unto God." (2 Nephi 26:33).
Even the jewels on our beach, that on
the surface seem to be striking in
their unique characteristics, are
alike to our Father in Heaven,
for He is no respecter of
persons, places, or
things.

Our beautiful beach
at Northwinds at Priest Lake
has been charitably described as 'the
eighth wonder of the world' as well as 'an
engineering feat of unprecedented proportion'. It
has also been a hot topic in both landscaping and
architectural journals, as well as in I.D.L. internal
memos and at monthly meetings of the Huckleberry
Bay H.O.A. Design Committee. The only reasonable
explanation for such interest as well as its longevity
is that we've received unanticipated assistance from
the Inhabitants of eternal worlds. They have run
interference for us, though we remain unaware
of Their proximity and accessibility, not to
mention Their immeasurably protective
influence over our beach and in our
behalf. In the face of daunting
obstacles, it is because of
Them that we live, and
move, and have
our being.

On cold winter
nights, we raise our eyes
to the cosmos and see among
the brightly illuminated stars a
trail created by God to help us find our
way back to our celestial Home. The jewels
on our beach remind us that this sparkling
multi-faceted pathway of diamonds was set in
the heavens to guide us to the infinite reaches of
eternity. Its starlight provides the clarity we need
to maintain our bearings while negotiating the
landscapes of our terrestrial lives. As it shines
on our hopeful countenances, we realize that
Priest Lake is our crown jewel, and is a
prototype of the heavenly mansions
that have been prepared for us.

The jewels that we cast upon our beach symbolize the armorial bearing that distinguishes us as representatives of a royal family. In the circumstances that are dictated by the principles of God's Plan, we become one with a universe that has embraced its divine destiny to become a living, breathing entity. It has received its spiritual quickening to become a neo-natal incubator "for the making of Gods." (Henri Bergson).

Among
God's countless
creations scattered across
an infinite number of galaxies
throughout the cosmos, our experiences
on Earth building beaches and scattering
jewels are not just inconsequential dry runs.
They are not like dress rehearsals for Broadway
plays that abruptly close after receiving bad press
on opening night. In virtually every star system in
each of the galaxies throughout Creation, the drama
that is Heavenly Father's perfect Plan of Happiness
has instead received Oscars and Golden Globes for
best screenwriting, visual effects, choreography,
writing, music, production, sound, design,
and best picture and Director.

Stars are nuclear
fusion reactors. Every second
of every minute of every day, our
Sun converts about 600 million tons
of hydrogen into helium. This process
takes place in its core, where photons, the
elementary quanta of radiant energy,
are released that take up to 250,000
years to reach its surface. Then,
in just 8 minutes, they travel
to Northwinds as sunshine
that caresses our cheeks
to a golden tan as we
enjoy the warm
sand on our
beach.

The work
of Woodland Elves
may be like that of the
Seven Dwarfs, who marched
off to toil in their diamond mine,
loudly singing as they went: "Hi ho,
hi ho, its off to work we go. We dig in our
mine the whole day through. It is what we
like to do." It may be that our children are
the fortunate beneficiaries of the nightly
endeavors of fairy creatures who have
scattered the jewels that magically
appear across our beach nearly
every morning during
the summer.

Six times in
the brief account in
Genesis of the Creation
of the Earth, our Father in
Heaven described His work
as good. The scriptures don't
divulge His feelings about the
construction of our beach. But
our practical and artistic efforts
must be good in His eyes, since
we have not only been given fire
for the deed, but we have also
felt the influential power
of divine intervention.
Soli deo gloria.

We discover
our superpowers,
such as the magical
resupplying of jewels
to our beach, when we
have participated in
quality one-on-one
time with the
cosmos.

Did our Heavenly Father randomly fashion the Crown Jewel of North Idaho? Was it only an afterthought? Did He sanction the creation of our beach at Northwinds on a whim, or was it accomplished by inspiring us to respect His Divine Design? "Everyone who is seriously interested in the pursuit of science," declared Albert Einstein, "becomes convinced that a Spirit is manifest in the laws of the universe. God doesn't play dice with His creations." He didn't leave the creation of things as beautiful as our lake to chance. He also created you, His magnum opus, on purpose. The next time a gentle breeze blows out of the south, try to remember that He is the wind beneath our wings.

In our efforts to
understand the complexity
of the human genome, we may
yet discover within the fascinating
matrix of the double helix the blueprints
of an interstellar family tree. The far end of
that scale may contain a galactic equivalent
of "Family Search" waiting for us to activate
our subscription. As the dog Frank, in the
motion picture "Men in Black", observed:
"You humans are always looking for
the spectacular. Try looking for
something very small,
like a jewel."

Pure hearts,
clean hands, and
willing minds alert
our Heavenly Father to
reach out and quicken
the gemstones that,
beforehand, He has
scattered across
the beaches of
our lives.

If my memory serves me correctly, I believe that it was Sir Isaac Newton who famously declared something along these lines: "I don't know what I may appear to the world, but to myself I seem to have been only like a boy playing on the shoreline at Northwinds, and diverting myself now and then by finding a prettier jewel or finer sand than ordinary, while the lake of truth lay undiscovered before me."
☺

As
we relax
on our beach
during a lazy
summer afternoon,
every now and then we
need to look up, because
outer space is never more
than 62 miles above our
heads, and eternity may
be even closer than
that.

The softening influence of lake time is good therapy for hard hearts and stiff necks. Malleability and pliancy are cultivated by the spiritual reconciliation that is the signature of the country North of The Narrows and that is amplified by quality time that we spend on our beach, getting better acquainted with ourselves, with each other, and with Mother Nature Herself.

From the
perspective of our beach, as
we contemplate the stars wheeling
across the night sky, we arrive at an
epiphany relating to opposition in all
things. We realize that the universe,
that is spread out before us in the
panorama of the Milky Way, is
so well balanced that the very
fact that we have problems
suggests that there are
solutions yet to be
discovered.

There is
something about our
beach at Northwinds that
binds our heartbeats to
the majestic rhythm
of the cosmos.

May
we be so
bold to say
that our beach
at Northwinds
has a copyright
on children's
fairytales?

It is
right here
at Northwinds,
beneath the Milky
Way's spectacular star
studded canopy, that we
are introduced by the Spirit
to the perspective of heaven. It
invites us to take our bearings
on eternity, and to see things as
they really are. It encourages us to
loose the latchets from our shoes, as
we reverently venture into sacred
precincts that are the province
of a heady influence that
can only be described
as the mind of
God.

Endless
creative possibilities are
catalyzed by the summer storms
that pound our beach at Northwinds.
We recall a multitude of questions that
we had never before thought to ask, and our
senses are overwhelmed with understanding
as we sit together on the shores of the lake. As
we venture into undiscovered country North
of The Narrows of our minds, expanding
awareness enlarges our comprehension
to unprecedented proportion.

If, as Longfellow observed: "Music is
the universal language of mankind," then
the consonant rhythm that is found at Priest
Lake, and that we hear so clearly from our beach at
Northwinds, unmistakably quickens the chords of
understanding. Those of us who have heard these
resonating patterns, not just with our ears, but
also with our hearts, know what Einstein
meant, when he declared: "I see my
life in terms of music."

The uplifting music
of children's laughter graces
our beach with a calming influence
that draws us into the embrace of the
spirit Of Priest Lake. As Plato observed:
"Music is a moral law that gives soul to
the universe, wings to the mind, flight to
the imagination, and charm and gaiety
to life." We hear cosmic harmony in
the simple declaration of Hans
Christian Anderson: "When
words fail, music
speaks."

Countless times, we
have stood in awe of the power
and majesty of God, Whose thunder
and lightning storms have wheeled across
the lake, streaked over our heads, and splashed
and crashed above us on the Selkirk Crest. David
described a similar occasion when the Lord came
from heavenly glory and inserted Himself into
his everyday world: "Fire (went) before (Him
and) His lightnings enlightened the world.
The earth saw, and trembled. The hills
melted like wax at the presence of
the Lord of the whole earth."
(Psalms 97:3-5).

Our dogs, and especially our beloved Katie, Danner, and Mackensie, have completed our lake experience. Northwinds would have had an entirely different character without them. "If there are no dogs in heaven," Will Rogers rightly declared, "then when I die, I want to go where they went."

None of us
has yet plumbed the
true depths of our abilities.
However, we know that potential
energy is linked to position, while
kinetic energy is related to motion.
In anticipation of the opportunities
that the new dawn might bring, we
position ourselves at Priest Lake,
advantageously at Northwinds,
and squarely on our beach, to
be ready to answer the call
as soon as it comes, and
then to move forward
with purpose and
confidence.

We are
fortunate to have
created a treasury of
remembrances at Priest
Lake, for "the life given us
by nature, is short. But the
memory of a life well
spent is eternal."
(Cicero).

At Northwinds,
we're on 'lake time'
which suggests that we
measure the progress of our
days largely by the position
of the Sun as it makes its way
across the sky. 'Lake time' is not
a predator that forever stalks us. It
is, instead, our traveling companion
reminding us to cherish each moment
of every day. It gauges our approach
to an event horizon beyond which
lies the undiscovered country
of eternity.

There are
as many atoms in
one molecule of our D.N.A.
as there are stars in the Milky
Way. As we stare up at the night
sky, taking in the ether that infuses
God's cosmos with energy, we sometimes
forget that each of us is a tiny universe
that contributes, in its own way, to a
celestial nobility that manifests
its armorial bearing with an
overstatement that is
intergalactic in
scale.

Our Father in
Heaven introduced the
mercurial element of time into
our experiences at Priest Lake, and
then decreed that its arrow should move
in only one forward direction. In order to
maintain its coherence while it lingered at
Northwinds, He meticulously apportioned it
in discrete increments, including seconds,
minutes, hours, and so on. It was a stroke
of genius that has allowed thought and
feeling, not to mention creativity and
spontaneity, to germinate with its
passage, all the while nurtured
within the fertile matrix of
free will.

The James Webb Space
Telescope has been endowed with
unprecedented sensitivity that will give
it the power of a cosmological time machine.
This will help astronomers compare the faintest
and earliest galaxies to today's breathtaking
spirals and ellipticals. It will also enlarge
our understanding of how Priest Lake
formed 12,000 years ago. In a way,
it, with the lake, helps reconcile
time with eternity.

North of
The Narrows, at one
time or another, we have all
knelt in awe of God's miracles
and wondered why His interactions
with His children are so often spectacular.
It must be because He belongs to eternity, and
thus, He introduces us to celestial phenomena that
are alien to our physical universe. Examples include
laws that relate to His perception of time, which for
Him is much more than a fluid medium. It is a
dynamic and rushing torrent, splashing in
all directions and slapping on every rock
of His creations, and even forming
temporal distortions, or ripples
in the sand along the
shorelines of our
lives.

At Priest Lake,
we learn that the stars are
majestic astronomical wonders that
give hope to the billions who wish upon
them. From the heavens, we receive the
gift to see, not only others, but also
ourselves more charitably, and
in a more benevolent light.
And that is a very
good feeling,
indeed.

At Northwinds, we are enveloped within the warm embrace of heaven, that we might live "under the glance of the piercing eye of the Almighty God." (Jacob 2:10). It is here that we clearly hear His voice, for it "is unto all, and there is none to escape, and there is no eye that shall not see, neither ear that shall not hear, neither heart that shall not be penetrated." (D&C 1:2).

As
we mature,
and as our faltering
steps become more confident,
we recognize the wisdom of Hans
Christian Anderson, who said: "Our
lives are fairy tales waiting to be written
by the finger of God." Many of the chapters in
our personal journals have already been completed,
and we don't know how many pages remain. But we do
know this: Although we cannot start over and make a new
beginning, we can begin now and write a new ending. We
believe God when He says: "If your eye be single to my glory,
your whole bodies shall" become as jewels that are "filled with
light." (D&C 88:67). Jewels that are bursting with light are
of God, and those who are of Him "receiveth light, and
continueth in (Him, and) receiveth more light;
and that light groweth brighter and
brighter until the perfect day."
(D&C 50:24).

Bathed in the glory
of the Lord, Moses stood "in the
presence of God, and talked with him
face to face." (Moses 1:31). As he did so, he
was able to see "the inhabitants (of Northwinds),
and there was not a soul which he beheld not; and he
discerned them by the Spirit." (Moses 1:28). Clearly, the
Lord sees not as we do, for we look only upon "the outward
appearance," while the Lord focuses on the inner vessel, on
every individual grain of sand that makes up the beaches
of our lives, which is beyond our capacity. (1 Samuel
16:7). We understand why He has said that He
"can stretch forth (His) hands and hold all
the creations which (He has) made, and
((the beaches that He has) made, and
(His) eye can pierce them" all.
(Moses 7:36).

Northwinds has always held
us within its embrace, to energize our
innate longing to apprehend the visions of
the eternal world. Our sandy deposits on the
beaches of our lives symbolize our progression
toward the distant mileposts that mark the way
each of us must go as we journey on toward our
destiny. The waves that have crashed upon the
boulders we've protectively placed along their
shorelines have become the familiar refrains
of a celestial symphony that first caught
our attention and piqued our spiritual
curiosity during our primeval
childhood, and that now
holds us firmly in
its grasp.

The endless yards of sand, gravel, and
rock that have generationally contributed to the
shoreline of Priest Lake are tangible representations of
the core curriculum of a school of hard knocks. Awakening
memories suggest that we had been strangers on our beach. We
had wandered from a more exalted sphere where we had received
the commission to restore purity, as best we could, to a lone
and dreary world that had been devoid, for far too long,
of delightful sand-castle sanctuaries. These, we were
told, would have the power to restore the optimism
of youth, give tired lungs a second wind, and
energize God's children to feel that life
would be worth living, and that
eternal life would be worth
dying for.

For over a quarter of a century, we have navigated the lake's turbulent waters, but we have always returned to the sanctuary of our dock at Northwinds. From our beach, we have engaged in lively conversations and identified the perils, pitfalls, and minefields of mortality. We have mapped out success strategies that have blessed us with safe passage while negotiating the twists and turns of East Shore Road, and while avoiding the cavernous perceptual potholes that have always been present on the figurative highways and byways of life.

Though our beach may
have accomplished little else,
it has symbolized our celebration
of life. It has been our first-aid station
where we have been treated when we have been
wounded by fiery darts, and a safe haven from
the cares of the world. It has beckoned us to grasp
the horns of sanctuary. It is where we have found
a healing balm to massage our aching spiritual
muscles, and it is where we have been taught
the order of heaven. Our beach has served
as a prototype of how and where we
would like to spend eternity.

Family members
who are familiar with the
never-ending drama related to our
beach construction and preservation
have seen, not frivolous repetition, but
instead, theatrical encore in its endless
iterations. They have been witnesses to our
active and vital engagement with life. Our
beach has provided us with much more than
fleeting opportunities to have our moments
in the Sun. The very core of our being has
been illuminated and energized by the
sustaining influence of a spiritual
awakening that gives vitality to
the God-given potential that
has always been present
within each of us.

How ever our small strip of sand may fit into the grand scheme of the cosmos, we do know that our Father in Heaven "lends (us) breath, that (we) may live and move and do according to (our) own will, and (He supports us) from one moment to another." (Mosiah 2:21). It is our faith that our efforts to create a beachhead at Northwinds have received His divine approbation.

Our beach at
Northwinds has allowed
us to reacquaint ourselves with
God's Divine Design and to put the
finishing touches on our dissertations
on life. Each bag of sand has contributed
to our magnum opus that emulates His
work and glory. It has blessed us with a
lucidity that comes from the heart and
not from the head, and it reminds us
of the peaceful setting back in our
heavenly Home, as well as of the
premortal instructions that so
gently massaged our spirits
as we readied ourselves for
arrival at what would
become our heaven
on Earth.

In all our favorite fairy tales, we read the hopefully optimistic concluding line: "… and they all lived happily ever after." However, that promise hasn't been etched in the sand on our beach. Instead, at Northwinds, the sparkling jewels that magically appear on summer mornings to catch the rays of the sun provide just a foretaste of the happiness that has been prepared for us, and that waits just beyond the far horizon. The fulfilment of God's promises waits entirely upon our initiative.

Prior to the construction of our
beach at Northwinds, we had not "found pure space,
nor seen the outside curtains, where nothing has a place."
Only after it had taken its shape thanks to our blood, sweat,
toil, and tears, did we comprehend that there is no end to
matter, space, spirit, or race; virtue, might, wisdom, or
light; union, youth, priesthood, or truth; glory, love,
or being. It is along the shoreline of Priest Lake
that we began our real education, the scales
of darkness fell from our eyes, and we
started to see things as they really
are. (See: W. W. Phelps, "If
You Could Hie to
Kolob").

It is in the next act of life's Three
Act Play that all of the mysteries relating to
the construction of our beach will be revealed, and
all the pieces relating to the puzzle of its maintenance
will fall into their proper places. All the uncertainty that had
perplexed us regarding its preservation will be assuaged. Every
variable relating to the conservation of its natural resources
and dimensional stability will be identified and managed
appropriately. Our beach may yet withstand the tests of
time and witness the millennial reign of Christ. Who
knows? Its building specifications may allow it
to endure throughout all eternity, (although
that may be a stretch).

The tranquil environment
at Priest Lake, as well as its timeless
nature, belie the fact that mortality is but a
very small sliver of a much larger slice of life.
We are molded during our mortal sojourn, but
we are established in eternity, and one fine
day will be encircled about by heavenly
smiles and will enjoy the steady beat
of the same rhythms that so often
touched our heartstrings as we
savored life from our
sandy beach.

In the turbulent
wake of stormy weather, we
have recognized our repetitive efforts
to repair our beach as nothing more than
pop quizzes in the learning laboratory of life.
It is in those difficult circumstances that we have
been blessed to see the bigger picture, and to view our
labors as an investment in relationship capital as we
prepare ourselves for the inevitable accounting that
awaits each of us following the conclusion of a
mortal curriculum that has been principally
involved in reconciliation, restoration,
restitution, and recommitment,
leading to renewal.

In the beginning, our beach was without form and was void. But as it was transformed into its current state, it was always my goal to establish a balance with nature and a state of harmony with both heaven and earth. As we worked together, I was often comforted by the Savior's promise: "I will go before your face. I will be on your right hand, and on your left, and my Spirit shall be in your heart, and mine angels," your children and grandchildren, will be "round about you, to bear you up."
(D&C 84:88).

The
Milky Way, our
parent galaxy, is like a
mother, since she gives birth to
stars. Each one we see is its child.
Every planet, that we cannot see, is its
grandchild. Northwinds, then, must be
its favored great-grandchild. In the end,
observed Neil Tyson, "we are connected
to each other biologically, to the Earth
chemically, and to the rest of the
universe atomically. We are
part of the universe."

The time we
spend on our beach
detoxifies us from the cares
of the world. Our advancing years
leave us heavy with anticipation, eagerly
looking forward to the third act of life's Three
Act Play, and becoming familiar with the final
pages of the script, to live happily ever after in
a magical kingdom where the enchantment
never ends, and our dream really do
come true, after all.

When there are no more bags
of sand to add to the beaches of our lives,
and the last scattered jewels have been eagerly
gathered, the on-going task to secure our eternal
legacy will be complete. No winds will blow down
from the north country except they fill our sails. No
waves will undermine our fortifications of faith. No
gaps will appear in the lake-side wall of our family
history. There will be no names missing from the
book of life that has been carefully compiled by
the angels in heaven, and there will be no
empty seats around the table when we
all sit down together to enjoy our
reunion at family dinner in
our heavenly home.

*Building
our beach has helped us
in our efforts to re-establish a
close relationship with our Creative
Consultant, Guidance Counselor, and Job
Foreman. He has always been available to offer
constructive comments relating to our developing
storyboard at Northwinds. He has stood as a Sacred
Sentinel, extending a bejeweled invitation for us to
return to the easy familiarity of life beyond the
gates of heaven, and to discover His Rest. He
has been there to carry our burdens and to
revitalize us so that we might walk
and not be weary, and run
and not faint.*

The crystal-clear clarity of our
vision is sometimes clouded by cataracts that
are inevitably created as we make concessions to the
influences of the world. If we find ourselves pigeonholed by
a narrow perspective, we will be forced into making comfortless
compromises, leaving the landscapes of our lives dreary and empty
shells. We'll never enjoy the breathtaking vistas of Distillery Bay,
Ploughboy Mountain, Green Bonnet, Trapper Peak, or Mollies' and
Phoebes' Tips. If we don't allow 'lake time' to heal our wounds, our
prognosis for reconciliation must forever remain poor. At Priest
Lake, and especially when we are North of The Narrows, we
will discover heavenly therapy for eyes that have lost the
ability to see clearly. We will be drawn to our beach at
Northwinds because it provides inspiration that
more easily facilitates the restoration of
our sight to its natural and
native acuity.

In its many iterations, our beach
at Northwinds has been a testing center,
a learning laboratory, and a citadel of higher
education, where we have learned to cope with life's
storms that threaten to sweep us over the precipice of
destruction. Adorned as it is with a smattering of
jewels, it is a poor substitute for God's Rest,
and yet, it is a fair representation of our
crude attempt to recreate the familiar
stability and secure sanctuary
of our heavenly Home.

The lake
invites us
to live boldly,
abandon comfort
zones, disengage our
safety nets, and forsake
the ports of refuge to which
the timid have apprehensively
retreated at the very first sign of
danger, only to squeak out their
lives and to scurry about from
one shadowy sanctuary to
another, in a flight
from freedom.

From the shelter of our
beach, as we look out across the
lake during summer storms, we see
lightnings, and mountains smoking,
and perceive the voices of trumpets and
thunderings that speak to our souls
in language that is inarticulate
but irrefutable. It is in these
reverberations that we
hear the mind of
God.

We sit on our beach and look out across the lake, marveling at the way the storm clouds eddy north and then pinwheel out of the Upper Priest Lake basin. In awe of nature, we listen to the thunder rolling over the ridges of the Selkirk crest. We are witnesses to the only homing beacons that are powerful enough to penetrate the swirling mists of darkness that characterize our telestial world. These are as jewels on our beach, placed there to guide us safely past the rocky shorelines of our personal misfortunes. They lead to celestial bridges that arch heavenward, above and beyond the deviations of life to the steadiness of a kingdom that resides in quiet repose; one that is far from the madding crowd, that is above the instability and the turmoil of the world.

Like a will o' the wisp, the flickering lights of eternity have danced all around us while we've built our beach North of the Narrows. The forgotten features of immortality have once again been illuminated by a steady spiritual light as we've worked to create a little piece of heaven on earth, at Northwinds on Priest Lake.

"Until we built a cabin,
I never realized how many
brilliant stars dotted the night sky.
Until we built a cabin, I couldn't really
see how wonderous God's creations are, and
what they mean to me. Until we built a cabin,
I don't think I understood what blessings would
be given us within those shady woods. And so,
we have a cabin, our family's to share, with
room enough within our hearts for the
memories we'll make there."
(Joanna Hudson
Oldham).

About The Author

Phil and Jan
Hudson raised 7 children and
were blessed with 26 grandchildren. They
particularly enjoyed being with their family
at their cabin nestled in the Selkirk Mountains,
on the eastern shore of Priest Lake, the crown jewel
of North Idaho. Phil had a successful dental practice
in Spokane, Washington for 43 years, before retiring
in 2015. He had an eclectic mix of hobbies and enjoyed
the out of doors. He always found time, however, to
record his thoughts on his laptop, and understood
Isaac Asimov's response, when he was asked:
"If you knew that you had only ten
minutes left to live, what would
you do?" He answered:
"I'd type faster."

By The Author

Essays

    Volume 1 - Spray from The Ocean of Thought
    Volume 2 - Ripples on a Pond
    Volume 3 - Serendipitous Meanderings
    Volume 4 - Presents of Mind
    Volume 5 - Mental Floss
    Volume 6 - Fitness Training for the Mind and Spirit

First Principles and Ordinances Series

    Faith - Our Hearts are Changed
    Repentance - A Broken Heart and a Contrite Spirit
    Baptism - One Hundred and One Reasons Why We Are Baptized
    Holy Ghost - That We Might Have His Spirit to Be With Us
    Sacrament - This Do in Remembrance of Me

Minute Musings - Spontaneous Combustions of Thought

    Volume One
    Volume Two
    Volume Three

Book of Mormon Commentary

    Volume One - Born in The Wilderness
    Volume Two - Voices from The Dust
    Volume Three - Journey to Cumorah

Calendars

    In His Own Words - Discovering William Tyndale
    As I Think About the Savior
    Daily Inspiration from Scriptural Symbols

A Thought for Each Day of the Year

    Faith
    Repentance
    Baptism
    The Holy Ghost
    The Sacrament
    Life's Greatest Questions

Revelation
The Atonement
The House of the Lord
The Plan of Salvation
The Sabbath

Doctrine & Covenants Commentary

Volume One - Sections 1 - 34
Volume Two - Sections 35 - 57

Doctrinal Themes

Are Christians Mormon? - Volume One
Are Christians Mormon? - Volume Two
Are We Alone in The Universe? - Volume One
Are We Alone in The Universe? - Volume Two
Christmas is The Season When ...
Dancing With the Stars - Volume One
Dancing With the Stars - Volume Two
Dancing With the Stars - Volume Three
Dancing With the Stars - Volume Four
Dentistry in The Scriptures
Gratitude
Hebrew Poetry
Hiding in Plain Sight
One Hundred Questions Answered by The Book of Mormon
The Highways and Byways of Life - Volume One
The Highways and Byways of Life - Volume Two
The Highways and Byways of Life - Volume Three
The House of The Lord
Without the Book of Mormon
Writing on Metal Plates

Children's Books

Book of Mormon Hiking Song - Volume One
Book of Mormon Hiking Song - Volume Two
Book of Mormon Hiking Song - Volume Three
Happy Birthday
Muddy, Muddy
The Hiawatha Trail - An Allegory
The Little Princess
The Parable of The Pencil

The Strange Tale of Huckleberry Henry
The Thirteen Articles of Faith

The Last Book I'll Ever Write

Professional Publications

Diode Laser Soft Tissue Surgery – Volume One
Diode Laser Soft Tissue Surgery – Volume Two
Diode Laser Soft Tissue Surgery – Volume Three

These, and other titles, are available from online retailers.

Over the course of forty years and more, Phil wrote hundreds of essays whose subjects formed the basis for a wide variety of books, many of which were related to the Gospel. They included commentaries on the scriptures, calendars, thoughts for each day of the year, as well as children's books. He penned one volume about William Tyndale, and published a three-volume anthology about laser surgery in dentistry that became a standard in the profession. There was always another book in the planning stages whose working titles included: A Deal with the Devil, Dust to Dust, If You Could Hie to Kolob, Today is a Good Day to Die, Non-hybrid Seeds of Thought, Principled Priorities, Some Assembly Required, Glow in The Dark, Our Standing in the Polls, I Thought I'd Have More Time, If I Lose my Mind, Lost and Found, Misplaced Keys, No Illegal Aliens are Allowed in Heaven, Pick Up the Pace, Sunrise/Sunset, The Art of the Deal, The Great and Spacious Building, and When God Rested on the Seventh Day. But he pragmatically decided this volume would be the last book he'd ever write. It would be his magnum opus, to be published and distributed to his family after his death, and to be particularly enjoyed while at Northwinds.

Author's Note

If, as fate
would have it, my
passing precedes the completion,
publication, or distribution of this book,
I ask a favor of you and extend a challenge.
After you have received a copy, as you go through
each page, think about how I might have changed a
thought or added an anecdote, had I had the time
to do so. Add your own personalized notes to the
margins, and use your observations as food
for thought, should you one day return
to give those entries your further
attention.

Ave atque vale!

www.ingramcontent.com/pod-product-compliance
Lightning Source LLC
Chambersburg PA
CBHW062023050526
44107CB00106B/1013